# Spinning and Weaving

# Spinning and Weaving

by
Lynn Huggins-Cooper

PEN & SWORD
HISTORY

AN IMPRINT OF PEN & SWORD BOOKS LTD.
YORKSHIRE – PHILADELPHIA

First published in Great Britain in 2019 by
Pen & Sword History
An imprint of
Pen & Sword Books Ltd
Yorkshire – Philadelphia

ISBN 978 1 52672 452 6

A CIP catalogue record for this book is
available from the British Library.

Typeset in Ehrhardt 12/17 by
Aura Technology and Software Services, India
Printed and bound in England by TJ International Ltd, Padstow, Cornwall

Pen & Sword Books Limited incorporates the imprints of Atlas, Archaeology,
Aviation, Discovery, Family History, Fiction, History, Maritime, Military,
Military Classics, Politics, Select, Transport, True Crime, Air World,
Frontline Publishing, Leo Cooper, Remember When, Seaforth Publishing,
The Praetorian Press, Wharncliffe Local History, Wharncliffe Transport,
Wharncliffe True Crime and White Owl.

For a complete list of Pen & Sword titles please contact

PEN & SWORD BOOKS LIMITED
47 Church Street, Barnsley, South Yorkshire, S70 2AS, England
E-mail: enquiries@pen-and-sword.co.uk
Website: www.pen-and-sword.co.uk

Or
PEN AND SWORD BOOKS
1950 Lawrence Rd, Havertown, PA 19083, USA
E-mail: Uspen-and-sword@casematepublishers.com
Website: www.penandswordbooks.com

# Contents

# Introduction to Heritage Crafts

Heritage crafts are a part of what makes us who we are; part of the glue that has held families and communities together for centuries. That jumper your nanna knitted? A heritage craft. The willow basket made by your auntie? A heritage craft. Grandpa's hand turned pipe? Again, a heritage craft. These traditional crafts have been carried out for centuries, often handed down through families with a child learning the craft at a parent's knee. Heritage crafts are those traditional crafts that are a part of the customs and cultural heritage of the areas where they begin. A heritage craft is:

> 'a practice which employs manual dexterity and skill and an understanding of traditional materials, design and techniques, and which has been practised for two or more successive generations'.

*Radcliffe Red List of Endangered Crafts Report, Heritage Crafts Association 2017*

Heritage crafts are in trouble. The Heritage Crafts Association commissioned research into endangered crafts, supported by The Radcliffe Trust (http://theradcliffetrust.org/). The results make sobering reading. Greta Bertram, Secretary of the Heritage Crafts Association who led the research said:

> *The Radcliffe Red List of Endangered Crafts is the first research of its kind in the UK. We're all familiar with the idea of a red list of*

*endangered species, but this is the first time the methodology has been applied to our intangible craft heritage. While some crafts are indeed thriving, the research has shown that all crafts, and not just those identified as critically endangered, face a wide range of challenges to their long-term survival. When any craft is down to the last few makers it has to be considered at risk as an unpredicted twist of fate can come at any time.*

Some of the heritage crafts identified in the report are teetering on the brink of disaster, and could be lost during this generation. One hundred and sixty-nine crafts were surveyed and allocated a status of currently viable, endangered, critically endangered or extinct. The survey team spoke to craft organisations and craftspeople, heritage professionals and funding bodies, as well as members of the public.

Four crafts surveyed were seen as already extinct, having been lost in the last ten years: riddle and sieve making, cricket ball making, gold beating and lacrosse stick making.

Ian Keys, Chair of the Heritage Crafts Association, said:

*We would like to see the Government recognise the importance of traditional craft skills as part of our cultural heritage, and take action to ensure they are passed on to the next generation. Craft skills today are in the same position that historic buildings were a hundred years ago – but we now recognise the importance of old buildings as part of our heritage, and it's time for us to join the rest of the world and recognise that these living cultural traditions are just as important and need safeguarding too.*

An alarming seventeen more crafts are seen by the report as critically endangered and at serious risk. There are few artisans practising the crafts – sometimes there are just one or two businesses operating – and there are few or no trainees learning the craft anew as apprentices. So why do we find ourselves in this situation? At a time when a huge variety of crafts enjoyed as a hobby is booming and craft fairs pop up in every community centre, village hall and historic estate, it seems odd that traditional crafts are dying out. So why is there a problem?

The study found that for some of the endangered crafts, there was an ageing workforce with nobody young training, waiting in the wings to take over. For others, there were found to be few training courses, even if there were potential trainees. For some traditional crafters the problem was found to be a variety of economic factors. Cheap competing crafts from overseas have flooded the market and there is often an unwillingness of the part of the public to pay a fair price for items handmade in Britain, despite the craftsmanship involved and the high quality of products. Of course, most traditional craftspeople are running micro-businesses and it is increasingly difficult to run a small business in Britain with an increase in paperwork, red tape, rules and regulations. Add to this the quantity of bureaucratic tasks and marketing necessary for self-employment and that leaves scant time for honing and practising an artisanal craft.

The future of heritage crafts is threatened in Great Britain. Action needs to be taken now to reverse the trend and ensure that these heritage cultural traditions are not lost forever. So far, we are failing. Great Britain is one of only 22 countries out of 194 to not have ratified the 2003 UNESCO Convention on the Safeguarding of Intangible Cultural Heritage. This convention focuses on the non-physical aspects of heritage such as traditional festivals, oral traditions, performing arts and the knowledge and skills to produce traditional crafts. If governmental action is not taken soon, many heritage crafts will be consigned to history.

You can help by supporting heritage craftworkers with your wallet, and by attending demonstrations and events. You can also join the Heritage Crafts Association, even if you are not a heritage crafter yourself, to support the funding and research of heritage craft practices. At the time of writing, in 2017, it is £20 for an individual to join. *(http://heritagecrafts. org.uk/get-involved/)*

## Chapter 1

# Introduction to Spinning and Weaving

Fibre crafts have been around for nearly as long as people. Clothing, bedding, tents and other items made from textiles have always been of great importance for the survival and comfort of human beings. Without the ability to create yarn and weave it into fabric the world would be a cold and comfortless place. For millennia people have created fibre from plants and animal fur, spun them into skeins and woven them into garments and furnishings.

In the modern day we have access to all manner of fibres and fabrics with an explosion in textile development in the twentieth and twenty-first centuries and the development of laboratory and factory-created fibres, such as rayon, nylon, acetate and polyester. Whilst factory processes can spin fibre into yarn quickly, there has been resurgence in the desire for natural materials. The growth of the green movement, the move towards zero waste and finding ways to create materials with less impact on the environment has all had an impact. More people than ever are taking up the slower, mindful, earth-friendly crafts in an effort to create a more sustainable, less polluting way of life.

There has been massive growth in interest in processing fleeces, right from the alpaca or sheep's back, through skirting (removing the rather delightfully termed 'vegetable matter' that can mean anything from straw to poop!) and washing, to carding (brushing and blending on boards or with a carding machine) and spinning. Spinning is the name for the process whereby fibres are drawn out and twisted to create yarn, which can then be used for weaving, knitting and crochet. Many types of fibrous matter can be spun to make yarn: sheep, goat mohair, camel, yak and alpaca fleece can be used, as can hair from angora rabbits – and even fur tufts from domestic cats or dogs!

Plant fibre is also often spun, including cotton, hemp, nettle, soy, flax, bamboo, ramie and rose. Of course, silk fibre is spun using the cocoons of silk worms, and even 'sea silk' has been created from long filaments secreted by the *Pinna Nobilis* shellfish. The shellfish uses the threads to secure itself to the turbulent seabed, but skilled spinners have been able to create a most delicate fibre from the material.

Spinning is an important enough artisanal craft, historically speaking, that we have words in use today that were taken from spinning originally, but now have broader meanings. The *distaff*, or female line in genealogy comes from the tool used in spinning – and think about the use of the word *spinster*, to describe an unmarried woman. That comes from the Mediaeval era, when all the girls in a family would spin yarn to weave cloth and make clothes for the household. Myths and legends also feature spinning and weaving imagery – in Norse mythology, for example, the *norns* (the spinners of the threads of fate) are named for a word which in Old Norse means 'to twine'.

Weaving is the name given to the process of combining threads to make fabric on a loom. It involves interlinking a set of vertical threads – the warp – with a set of horizontal threads – the weft. In a plain weave, the weft thread goes over one warp thread and under the next. When the thread returns on the next row, it goes over the threads it previously went under, and under the threads it previously went over. This process continues until fabric is made.

We have had to find information about ancient textiles and the technology that made them via a patchwork of investigative archaeology, as little remains, relatively speaking, of the actual textiles themselves. Ancient clothing was made from organic materials such as cotton, wool and silk, and these are difficult to preserve; they rot and are subject to insect attack. Special situations, such as dry, salt-heavy conditions in some desert areas, as well as – amazingly – bog-like environments where lack of oxygen and bacterial growth prevents decay, have preserved enough ancient textiles to give us clues. Alongside ancient tools and carved and painted representations of people weaving and spinning, we are able to create a window into the past.

## Chapter 2

# Ancient Spinning and Weaving

People have been spinning fibre into yarn and weaving it into cloth since ancient times. Archaeological evidence suggests that spinning dates back to the Upper Paleolithic Era, over 20,000 years ago. Stones have been found, along with needles, suggesting they were used to spin fibre into yarn. Why would you produce needles if there were no fabric to sew together?

The earliest spinners probably rubbed downy fluff from animals up and 'spun' the down on their thigh with the flat of their hand, adding fluff to lengthen the piece, and thus creating yarn. The yarn would be attached to the stone, which would be twirled until the yarn was twisted and strong.

There is a great deal of archaeological evidence for textile work in the ancient world. As early as 8,000 BC there is evidence to show that flax was cultivated in the Near East. By 6,000 BC woven cloth was being used to wrap the dead in Anatolia. By 5,000 BC the Ancient Egyptians were producing linen cloth, as well as processing fibre made from rush, palm, reed and papyrus. By 3,000 BC there is evidence to show the farming of domesticated sheep with woolly fleeces in the Near East, and by 2,500 BC there is evidence that cotton was cultivated in the Indus Valley. As early as 298 AD there is evidence of the existence of a foot-powered loom at Tarsus.

Loom weights and spindle whorls are common finds at ancient sites and it is interesting to note that until recent times these were often overlooked as unimportant finds – strange, considering how vital textiles were for the survival and comfort of ancient peoples. It has been suggested by modern scholars that this lack of importance is as a result of much of textile history being the province of women and that 'women's work' was not seen as important. Of course, men may have been involved in the production of ancient textiles, but the view does perhaps have some merit.

Thousands of spindle whorls were found at Troy and huge baskets of them are on display at the Archeological Museum in Istanbul. We can learn a lot about ancient weaving practices from the patterns in which loom weights are arranged when they are found, particularly if there is evidence that the wooden looms were destroyed quickly by fire. If this happened, weights fell in rows and the arrangement gives us clues as to the structure of the cloth being woven.

Early looms were warp-weighted, simple wooden frames with warp threads hanging down, weighted by stones or similar. The frame would be fixed to wooden poles that could be driven into the ground or propped against a wall indoors. This type of loom was used from the Neolithic period, through the Roman era and beyond. The shuttle (the tool that carries the weft thread through the warp threads) was often a simple stick, with yarn wrapped around it. To facilitate the weaving and open the 'shed' – the set of threads – the weaver could hang the stone weights at different heights, or use heddles, where some threads were fastened to a stick for ease of movement. When the stick was moved, it moved some warp threads and opened the shed for ease of passage. The growing fabric would be 'beaten'; that is, a reed or stick would be used to compact the threads together as they were woven.

Spinning and weaving were an important part of a woman's life in Ancient Greece. The birth of a baby girl was announced by festooning the door post with wool roving as a sign of her gender. There are many depictions of women carrying out these tasks on pottery, in art and in writing from the time. Archaeological evidence of items that are in fact weaving and spinning tools can be helpfully contextualised by these artistic depictions.

The fact that goddesses and female mythological heroines were often shown weaving and spinning helps to show that it was a task held in high esteem. Athena was the goddess of women's crafts and weaving and spinning were the most important of these. The myth of Arachne, who was turned into a spider by Athena, tells of the woman's weaving skills. She makes the mistake of boasting that she is more skilled than Athena and, when she proves this in a contest, the capricious goddess wreaks her vengeance by transforming Arachne. The Fates are shown as spinners and weavers, drawing out – and cutting – the thread of men's lives. One of the three Fates, Clotho, was regularly depicted holding a spindle and distaff, which helps the modern world to understand how these tools were held and used.

Instead of the brushes, boards and carding machines used in the modern day, the ancient Greeks used a *kteis* to separate fibres. It was like a large comb. They also used an interesting tool called an *epinetron*, or *onoi*, which was a kind of 'thigh sleeve'. This was used to roll fibres to make roving, or *katagma*, ready for spinning. Mary Lois Kissell (1864–1944), the great anthropologist and pioneer of the cultural study of textiles, described these tools as being worn by Athenian women of rank 'like a great thimble' that fitted closely over the leg. The texture of the *onoi* would be raised, like fish scales, to help grip the fibre as it was rolled into roving. Interestingly, for a long time archaeologists, quite sensibly, thought *onoi* were some type of ornamental ridge roof tile – they look like them and are highly decorated. It was not until an *onoi* was found bearing an image of one on a woman's knee as she made roving that they realised what it was they were seeing. It also showed women spinning and weaving, washing wool and beating it to loosen the fibres – and the mystery object was recognised for what it really was. These tools were associated with the start of a young woman's role as a wife and they were often decorated with wedding scenes.

A distaff or *elakate* and spindle or *atrakto* – very similar to those used for hand spinning today – were used to spin yarn. The roving was wound onto the distaff and drawn out towards the spindle by hand to create thread. The distaff was often made from reed and the spindle was commonly made from saffron wood, a delightfully fragrant tool. The spindle had a hook at the top to hold the spun thread and a carved whorl or swirl at the bottom to make it easier to handle and control. Spindles were elegant, often decorated, and could be made from costly materials such as bronze, silver, ivory and gold. The Greek scholar Homer describes a golden distaff that was gifted to Helen of Sparta by Alexandra of Egypt and Theocritus is documented as giving an ivory spindle to the wife of his friend, Nicias of Milesia. The poet Catullus was moved to describe the process of spinning eloquently:

> *The loaded distaff in the left hand placed*
> *With spongy coils of snow white wool is graced*
> *From these the right hand lengthening fibres drew*
> *Which into thread, neath nimble fingers grew.*

*Chapter 3*

# Roman Spinning and Weaving

The Romans were fashion-conscious people and imported textiles, and the materials to create and dye them, from across their vast empire. Archaeological excavations at Pompeii have shown us a great deal about textiles in the ancient Roman world. It is estimated that there were around forty-three establishments producing textiles in the area, which suggests that the textiles were being made for export as well as local use. The graffiti in Pompeii has told us much about the ancient world and this is true for the textile businesses based here; one wall tells that there were two women spinning and five men weaving at the establishment. Another set of graffiti gives us the names of eleven spinners and five weavers. It was 'big business'.

Wall paintings give us more information. Most of the cloth made at Pompeii seems to have been made from wool, despite there not being evidence of great herds in the vicinity. That suggests that the wool required was imported. Remains suggest that white wool came from northern Italy; ginger wool from Asia Minor; tawny wool from Puglia and black from Spain. There was also grey wool from Cordoba. It is suggested that the demand for wool in the Roman Empire led to the development of sheep farming on a grand scale in Britain, as well as the large-scale development of the early textile industry. The workshops at Pompeii have evidence of wool preparation and dyeing, spinning and weaving.

Fascinating remnants of textiles in the area show us that fibres which have fallen out of common usage were spun and woven, such as ramie, from nettles – which is seeing something of a comeback in modern artisanal fibre circles – and poppy fibre. At Herculaneum there is a fragment of textile that was created using gorse fibre. Although this was still used in southern Italy until the twentieth century, it is not commonly used today.

Fibre and fabrics were also widely imported, including cotton from India and what is now Iraq, linen from Gaul, embroidered cloth from Asia Minor and fine muslin made from mallow fibre. Pliny the Elder writes about wild silk made from a native Mediterranean moth cocoon, but most silk at the time was imported from China to India along the Silk Road. It is interesting to note that Roman tastes did not favour heavy Chinese silk and much of it was unravelled and rewoven along with other threads such as cotton or linen to make a lighter airier weave. Paintings at Pompeii show the Roman love of diaphanous materials and these silk mixes fit the bill – as well as making expensive silk thread go further. Syrian and Egyptian weavers made gorgeous linen and silk mixes, including woven decoration and patterns.

There is also evidence of 'sea wool' at Pompeii, for the truly luxury end of the market in textiles. This was similar to the 'sea silk' of Ancient Greece, where the fibres from shellfish such as the *Pinna Nobilis* were gathered and woven into silky golden fabric. Lastly, a somewhat 'poison chalice', a fabric created from asbestos fibre. Rather tragically, both Greek scholar Strabo and Pliny the Elder remark upon the lung diseases suffered by slaves working with the material. It continued to be created into the mediaeval era, when it was charmingly called 'salamander fur', a reference to its fire-retardant quality.

Roman women spun using a 10-12 inch stick with a slit to catch the thread carved at the top. The lower end of the spindle was inserted into a small wheel or *vorticellum* which was made from wood, metal or stone. It kept the spindle steady and helped it to rotate as it was used.

Spinning was such an important 'womanly art' that spindles and distaffs were carried in bridal processions. There was even a goddess, Pallas, worshipped specially as the patroness of spinners.

*Chapter 4*

# Spinning and Weaving in Ancient Egypt

Flax spinning and weaving were important practices in Ancient Egypt. Flax was seen as a gift from the Nile, as the river flooded annually and left behind rich, fertile soil suitable for growing crops. Many wall paintings in tombs show its cultivation. It is a fast-growing plant, maturing at a height of 60 centimetres to a metre in a hundred days. Flax plants were gathered whilst in bloom, as the strongest fibre could be made from young plants; long fibres yielded from the plants were very strong. The plant fibre has high pectin content (the substance added to fruit puree in jam making to make it gel) and the sticky texture acts like a binder in damp conditions. Flax fibre dries quickly and resists rotting.

Once dried, the strips, containing twenty to forty strands, would be divided into usable sections. These sections were spliced together to form long lengths, twisted into roving then spun into yarn. Egyptian spinners often used two spindles simultaneously, with the balls of flax roving in a container on the floor. Some spinners stood on stools to maximise the height between the spindle and the ball of flax.

The yarn was then woven. Linen was woven on looms from around 5,000 BC, with evidence of paintings on pottery dating from this time showing looms and weavers at work. The linen produced was high quality and very fine. By 3,000 BC cloth was being created that had sixty-four warp threads and forty-eight weft threads per centimetre – an amazing achievement. By around 2,100 BC, during the sixth dynasty, it was said that cloth was so fine it could be drawn easily through a signet ring.

It is interesting to note that linen does not take dye as easily as some fabrics, and most ancient Egyptian linen was therefore a cream, or biscuit, colour in its natural state. However, green linen could be created when flax was harvested young, therefore wearing the colour green was a status symbol as the colour was strongest when the fabric was new.

Linen was used for clothing, bedding, furnishings and to make sacks and bags. Sails were made from it for boats, and nets for catching fish and birds were knotted together from the yarn. Linen was fashioned into slings for hunting small animals and birds and fibres were used to create fishing line and woven into rope. An ancient dentist from the Ptolemaic period, during the last centuries BCE, even used a wad of linen, presumably soaked in some type of painkiller or antiseptic-type substance, to pack a large area of tooth decay as a type of 'filling'.

Linen was as important for the dead as it was for the living. As corpses were mummified and anointed with oils, they were wrapped and swaddled in fine linen strips, soaked in resins and other preservatives. This wrapping gave the departed the protection of the goddess Tayet, the goddess of weaving. As it was made from recycled sheets and clothing, remains of mummy wrappings tell us a great deal about the textiles woven for everyday use in ancient Egypt. The idea of these linen bindings has given us the bandaged mummy beloved of Hollywood horror films. Linen was also, as a thing of value, often a part of funerary offerings. The tomb of a 17-year-old girl contained a wreath made from bound linen and the tomb of a prosperous woman who lived in around 1,500 BC contained three chests with an astounding seventy-six fringed linen sheets inside, including a 54 ft strip that may have served, when folded, as a mattress. Some had been mended and all were carefully laundered and pressed before folding ready for her journey into the afterlife.

Weaving and spinning were known throughout the ancient world. Indigenous Americans were skilled at spinning and weaving cotton.

The oldest example of weaving found in North America was discovered at the Windover archaeological site in Florida, with pieces dating back to 6,500 BC. In the South American Andes, people created yarn and gorgeously woven cloth from llama and alpaca wool, a fibre that is seeing resurgence among artisans today. By around 4,000 BC, these camelids were domesticated and farmed for their fleeces. The Incas wove beautiful pieces of textile which featured symbolic and religiously themed decorations. These were of practical use for clothing and furnishings, but they were also a way of demonstrating social class and rank. Textiles were even used as tributes and currency.

There is evidence to show that the spinning and weaving of silk from silkworm cocoons has taken place in China since around 3,500 BC, with silk fragments being excavated in tombs and burials. Evidence of silk weaving in Japan dates back to around 300 BC, and in Korea to around 200BC.

So, spinning and weaving was a feature of ancient civilisations around the globe. People first harvested the fibres found naturally in their locale and then farmed animals and fibre plants especially for spinning and then weaving into fabric. Cloth could be serviceable for work wear, or decorative for the higher classes in society. Costly fabrics made into clothing and furnishing spoke of rank; it allowed people to peacock their status.

Spinning and weaving were carried out using strikingly similar tools and equipment around the ancient world. Although some of this may be seen as due to migration and trade, it is interesting to explore the idea as to whether some of this similarity was down to parallel development of technology, due to similar designs being the most effective and efficient in the production of fabric.

*Chapter 5*

# Mediaeval Spinning and Weaving AD 476–1492

D uring the mediaeval period, hand spinning with a drop spindle was superseded by the invention of the spinning wheel. It was invented on the Indian subcontinent sometime between 500–1,000 AD with images showing its wide use in the Islamic world in the 1000s. It reached Europe via merchants from the Middle East.

This invention transformed lives. In most cultures around the globe, spinning and weaving took as much of women's time as growing and preparing food – so this was a game-changer. The spinning wheel produced yarn much faster than hand spinning, but it also produced uniform quality yarn more easily, as it added more 'twist' at finer places in the developing yarn and drew out thicker places. The spinning wheel increased productivity by more than ten times that of even the fastest hand spinners. Historian Lynn White has made the connection between the development of the spinning wheel and the increased production of cloth, to the supply of rags available and thus the development of cheap paper production. She claims that this had an effect in turn on the development of printing at this point in history. One developing technology acts as the 'mother' to other technologies in a web of connectivity.

In early Ireland spinning and weaving were seen as such important womanly skills that the *Brehon Laws*, set down between AD 600–800, decreed that in the case of a divorce, the woman should keep her wool bags, spindles, weaver's reeds and a portion of the yarn she had spun and the fabric she had woven.

Wool was the main fibre used in Europe in the Middle Ages, but linen and nettlecloth was used by poorer people. Cotton was used in Spain in the ninth century and moved across Europe. Weavers worked from home and took their cloth to sell at fairs. Warp-weighted looms as used by the ancients were still widespread until horizontal looms appeared in the tenth and eleventh centuries.

Weavers established guilds to protect and regulate their craft, which controlled the quality of cloth made and regulated training for those who wished to call themselves weavers.

Henry II granted the Weaver's Guild a charter that declared:

> *Know that I have conceded to the Weavers of London to hold their gild in London with all the liberties and customs which they had in the time of King Henry my grandfather.*

The charter allowed weavers the right to supervise the work of their craft, collect tax and to elect bailiffs. It could even control and police its members and had its own court. It was a powerful guild, as the cloth trade was of prime importance to the mediaeval economy. In the latter part of the Middle Ages, the weavers became less powerful as other textile-based merchant groups were formed, such as the cloth workers, haberdashers, drapers and mercers.

By the thirteenth century, things had changed dramatically. By 1200, spinning wheels and treadle looms were used widely in Europe, allowing even large tapestries – important for comfort in draughty buildings – to be woven. A system of 'putting out' was instituted, whereby the cloth merchant bought wool and provided it for the weavers, who then sold the woven fabric back to the merchant. This system controlled rates of pay and merchants became very prosperous. 'Wool towns' such as Norwich and Bury St Edmunds grew exponentially as a result of this new-found wealth.

In the fourteenth century there was great upheaval. The Hundred Years War took its toll on the population and there was bad weather followed by poor harvests. In 1346 the Black Death swept Europe and the population was almost halved. As a result there were not enough workers to till arable ground, land values fell and, with the sharp rise in labour costs, landowners looked for new ways to make their land pay. Sheep farming was the answer. Previously arable land was used as sheep pasture and traders from Bruges and Florence bought the wool. Arable land which had needed twenty to thirty men to work it could now be managed by a shepherd and a dog. In areas where wool could be produced and taken easily to ports for export, there was a boom in growth. The great 'wool churches' of East Anglia and the Cotswolds still stand as testimony to the fortunes that were amassed by sheep farming landowners.

These landowners also began to process wool themselves, outside the control of the guilds, and weavers began to move from their homes, where they had worked under the putting-out system, to purpose-built buildings, where working hours were regulated – a rudimentary factory system had begun. In the 1370s, Edward III began to tax raw wool exports and there was a shift as a result to export finished cloth rather than wool. During the late mediaeval period, the Crown earned forty shillings a sack for exported wool which was a huge amount. More capital was required for these overseas markets and wealth from the textiles industry began to be concentrated into fewer hands. Some cloth merchants employed hundreds of workers.

Horizontal frame looms with a treadle appear in European pictorial records from the thirteenth century and were highly developed. They were mounted in a frame and a foot-operated treadle moved the heddles. Shaft looms allowed weavers to set up as many as twenty-four shafts, enabling complex patterns to be woven. A batten replaced the old simple comb for beating the weft into place, and this made beating in easier and quicker. The foot-powered treadle freed the weaver's hands to throw the shuttle and swing the batten, speeding up the whole process. Basic looms stayed unchanged for centuries as they were so efficient in this form.

Intricate designs could require up to a hundred shafts and this kind of weaving was carried out on a draw loom. This type of loom probably first developed in the Far East for the weaving of finely figured silk fabric. It first arrived in Europe in the silk working centres of Italy during the Middle Ages. In addition to the shafts, which the weaver operated by treadles as on a basic loom, the draw loom had cords which were used to raise warp threads for the intricate weaving of patterns. The cords were controlled by a draw boy, who usually sat on top of the loom.

So, the mediaeval era was a time of rapid development of spinning and weaving, in terms of technological advancement. It saw the development and adoption of the use of spinning wheels as opposed to drop spindles and the like, which led to the efficiency of spinning increasing exponentially. The period also saw an increase in the world fabric trade and the formation of guilds to protect the rights of artisans within the trade. This would continue to evolve as the Tudor Age dawned.

*Chapter 6*

# Tudor and Stuart Spinning and Weaving 1485–1603

Gervase Markham's 1623 book of advice to women, *Countrey Contentments* or *The English Huswife: containing the Inward and Outward Vertues which ought to be in a Compleate Woman*, listed the virtues of a woman who could spin and weave to clothe her family:

> *Our English Huswife, after her knowledge of preserving and feeding her family, must learn also how, out of her own endeavours, she ought to clothe them outwardly and inwardly.*

The Tudor and Stuart era housewife needed to be able to spin and weave, or her family would have no clothes or bedding. Most yarn was made from flax, hemp or wool. He went on to say:

> *After your wool is thus mixed…you shall then spin it up on great wool wheels, according to the order of good housewifery.*

Tudor clothes and fashion varied strictly according to the social class and status of the wearer. Under the *Sumptuary Laws* or *Statutes of Apparel*, poor people were only permitted to wear wool, linen or sheepskin – never the richer fabrics such as silk, cloth of gold or silver, or velvet. The rank of a person was immediately recognisable from the clothes they wore.

The reason for the introduction of these laws was to control and subdue the newly wealthy and burgeoning merchant class. These men, from outside the nobility, could afford to buy luxury goods that had previously been reserved for the upper classes. Henry VIII had decided to maintain control of this growing class by creating laws to keep them in their place. Sumptuary Laws had existed since the Middle Ages, but they had been neglected and not strictly adhered to as a result of the effects of the Black Death, when the population had been reduced and labour became expensive. This caused a hike in social mobility as working people – even peasants – moved to towns and took up employment to fill gaps left by the plague. Trade flourished, the merchant class was born – and it had money to spend.

Henry also controlled the rich wool trade closely. In 1532 the export of wool to the continent was at first discouraged and then banned. This meant that wool remained in England to be spun and woven into cloth. The fabric created was lighter textured than the broadcloth of the mediaeval period. Fine woollen worsted, dyed red with madder, was made into petticoats and skirts and Kersey weight woollen cloth was dyed blue with indigo for everyday wear. Kersey was a coarse, hard-wearing cloth with a napped back that made it warm for the wearer, so it was ideal for working in.

From the 1560s onwards Huguenot refugees from Catholic countries such as France, Belgium and Holland poured into England. Many of these were silk weavers and lace makers and their skills helped to develop the textile industry in England. They also brought with them the weaving of serge, a type of twill-weave fabric that was relatively cheap to produce and made excellent hardwearing working clothes. In 1685, with the Edict of Nantes introduced by Louis XIV, French Protestants, particularly from Lyons and Tours, poured into England in large numbers. These Huguenot refugees brought with them their skills in weaving fine silks and they settled in Spitalfields in London. According to the French Committee in a report published in 1688, 13,050 French refugees had settled in London, mainly in Spitalfields. The editor of *Stow's Survey of London* wrote about Spitalfields and the weavers who lived there:

*Here they have found quiet and security and settled themselves in their several trades and occupations; weavers especially. Whereby God's blessing surely is not only brought upon the parish by receiving poor strangers, but also a great advantage hath accrued to the whole nation by the rich manufactures of weaving silks and stuffs and camlets, which art they brought along with them. And this benefit also to the neighbourhood, that these strangers may serve for patterns of thrift, honesty, industry, and sobriety as well.*

The French silk weavers manufactured watered silks, black mantuas, waltered tabies, ducapes, satins, velvets, brocades and strong silks known as pasuadoys. They also wove fabrics blending silk and cotton. These fabrics had previously only been available from France, but now the skills needed to produce them were permeating the weaving community in London. A weaver named Mongeorge brought a technique from Lyons that created a silk taffeta with a gorgeous lustre. Previously, the manufacture of lustrings for 'English taffeta' had been a lucrative export market for French weavers; now the fabric could be produced on English soil. In 1692 the Royal Lustring Company was set up by charter.

At the beginning of the sixteenth century the Saxony wheel was introduced into Europe. It had a bobbin that the yarn was wound on continuously and the distaff became a stationary rod. The wheel was turned by a treadle which freed the spinner's hands. This sped up production, as the spinner did not have to keep stopping to wind yarn.

Elizabeth I added to her father's *Sumptuary Laws* once she came to the throne. A proclamation of 1597 declared that only royalty and earls could wear cloth of gold or purple silk; nobody below the role of knight could wear long silk stockings called *netherstocks*; a baron's wife (but nobody below her rank) could wear gold or silver lace and, with a strange level of detail, only the eldest son of a knight (but not his younger brothers) could wear velvet doublet and hose. Furs were similarly controlled; Elizabeth and her alleged paramour the Earl of Leicester were the only people allowed to wear sables, for example. Contravening these laws held stiff penalties, yet prostitutes often flaunted them, wearing elaborate garments made from costly fabrics, like high-ranking ladies.

For everyone lower down the social scale in Elizabethan times, from peasants to merchants, wool was worn. That does not mean that their clothes were inferior quality; wool was woven into many types of fabric. Everything from heavy coat fabric, to brocade, veiling and velvet were woven from wool. Gowns, coats, capes, tunics, jerkins, doublets and sleeves would be made from wool. Undergarments, such as smocks and chemises were made from finely woven linen – like today's 'handkerchief linen' in terms of softness. Many dresses were lined with linen, even for high class women. Peasants would wear smocks made from heavy linen with a thick weave.

The wool industry was a massive and powerful affair in Tudor times. Many people owned small flocks of around twenty to thirty sheep, alongside other professions. Large landowners could own massive flocks, such as Sir Henry Fermor, who left flocks numbering 15,500 sheep when he died in 1521. During the sixteenth century, the government set a limit on the number of sheep that could be owned by individuals, setting the cap at 2,400. They also created the curious rule in 1555 that sheep could not be kept to the exclusion of other animals, with the proviso that for every sixty head of sheep, a milking cow had to be kept. Sheep – or more precisely, their wool – were big business. Between 1450 and 1550 the price of wool doubled. This does not sound like a large rise over a hundred years until it is compared to the price of grain, which remained at the same level until the 1520s.

In 1454, Parliament declared: …*the making of cloth within all parts of the realm is the greatest occupation and living of the poor commons of this land.*

The majority of the Crown's income came from tax duties on wool and cloth – a stunning thought.

By the 1540s there was massive inflation and the price of raw wool was artificially high. The value of a fleece was decided by a combination of weight and the type of wool produced. In 1600 the best wool in England was produced by Ryeland sheep in Herefordshire, Shropshire and Staffordshire, on the Welsh border. This fine, heavy fleece was referred to as 'Lemster Ore' and was prized above all other breeds both domestically and in trade on the continent. It had a long fine staple (hair length) and was particularly suited to the production of worsted material, a fine suiting.

The English Civil War (1642–1651), and the austerity of the Protectorate under Oliver Cromwell that followed, made for leaner times for the producers of luxury goods such as finely-worked cloth.

When Charles II was restored to the throne in 1660 there was a magnificent and opulent parade in the City of London. Liverymen lined the streets in their decorative and expensive robes. However, relief at the restoration of the monarchy was short lived for the merchants, as the Great Plague swept through London, killing a third of the population. Trade ground to a halt as people fought to survive. Cripplegate, Southwark and Whitechapel, where the weavers were concentrated, were areas where the plague struck hardest. Another blow was to follow. Just as London began to recover from the worst of the epidemic, the Great Fire of London roared through the city, destroying the livelihoods of thousands as well as taking a terrible toll on the people. During the fire the great Weaver's Hall was burned to the ground.

The Tudor and Stuart period had seen great changes for the textile industry. The rise of the rich merchant classes had given rise to a series of bizarre, to modern eyes at least, Sumptuary laws that decreed the types of fabric and clothing that could be worn by different classes and echelons of society. Wave after wave of refugees from the continent, such as the Huguenots, brought new methods and techniques with them to England, enriching the textile trade as a result. The wool trade saw heady heights of profit and then slumped due to massive taxation and loss of markets. It survived the Civil War and then flourished during the Restoration, only to suffer, along with other artisanal trades, as a result of the terrible period in the 1660s that encompassed The Great Plague and the Great Fire of London. Turbulent times!

## Chapter 7

# Georgian Era Spinning and Weaving 1714–1837

The Georgian era was a time of massive expansion in the textile industry. Across Britain, mills produced fine woollen, linen, cotton and silk cloth. Technological advances were being made thick and fast and the variety of fabrics being woven grew year by year. The silk industry, for example, which had been boosted massively by the influx of Huguenots to Spitalfields in the Mediaeval and Tudor periods, continued to advance into the Georgian era. Sir Thomas Lombe brought the Italian technique of organzining raw silk for weavers to England and was granted a patent in 1718. Organzining prepared the silk ready to be used and made the production of silk fabric cheaper. The technique was also later adopted by the cotton industry.

Perhaps encouraged by the growing success of the silk trade, a man charmingly named John Appletree tried something amazing in London in 1718: he started a silk farm in Chelsea. He wanted to free the English silk trade from having to import raw silk from the continent by farming silkworms on an industrial scale. This ambitious plan was granted a patent and Appletree produced a prospectus about the project, inviting the general public to subscribe to The Raw Silk Undertaking for the huge sum of a million pounds – a Georgian crowdfunding project!

Appletree, encouraged by natural history writer and local resident Henry Barnham, created a silkworm plantation in a walled park in Chelsea. Chelsea Park had once been part of Sir Thomas Moore's land, attached to his Tudor mansion by the Thames. This land was known historically as 'the Sand Hills' and remained arable and pasture land well into the eighteenth century. The site was a good one; exotic plants were already being grown at the Chelsea Physic Garden, which had been established in 1613 on the banks of the Thames. Appletree was granted a sixty-year lease of the site in 1718 by Sir William Sloane and he planted an amazing 2,000 black and white mulberry trees.

Appletree took out a patent on an 'evaporating stove' which was to keep the silkworm eggs at a constant warm temperature. He built houses to incubate the eggs and raise the silkworms, as well as accommodation for harvesting the silk from the cocoons. He also created a system to supply the silkworm larvae with the dry mulberry leaves they required to feed upon, even when it was raining. At first the project flourished; satin fabric was woven from the silk and made into gorgeous dresses presented to Caroline of Ansbach, the Princess of Wales. Despite this, by early 1724 the business was foundering. The silk was expensive to produce in the harsh British climate and in 1721 Walpole had removed import tax on raw silk, making it hard for a domestic project to compete with cheap raw silk from the colonies in East India. In May John Appletree was declared bankrupt.

After Appletree's business failed, Sloane granted the lease of the park to Sir Richard Manningham who uprooted most of the trees. Chelsea Park was broken up into lots and sold off. The dream was over.

A few of the old mulberry trees remain and can still be seen in Chelsea today. One stands in a private communal garden and another grows on the eponymous Mulberry Walk, another stands in the courtyard of Argyll Mansions.

In 1781 Richard Arkwright founded the world's first steam-driven mill in Manchester. The arrival of steam power and the mechanisation of the industry that followed, built great towns like Manchester, and the textile industry was a foundation for its wealth. Textiles could finally be truly mass produced.

Until the 1740s all spinning was still done by hand, mostly on a spinning wheel. Carding and spinning might be the only employment a family had, or they may have farmed a few acres and also worked with wool and cotton fibre. To contextualise, it took around three carders to produce enough roving for one spinner and around three spinners to provide yarn for one hand weaver. Handloom weavers would then take fabric to market and offer it for sale. The process was continuous and all the members of the family, both sexes, from the youngest to the oldest would take part.

By the 1740s things were changing and *fustian masters* would give out raw materials to weavers and then would collect the finished cloth under the *putting out* system. The fustian master would then arrange to dye the finished cloth and take it to shop keepers to be sold.

Things changed again with mechanisation. In 1738 two Birmingham-based men, John Wyatt and Lewis Paul, patented their 'Roller Spinning Machine' – which used two sets of rollers that travelled at different speeds, to create a yarn with even, consistent thickness. They opened a mill in 1742 and used a donkey to power their machine. It was not a successful venture. In 1743, a factory using five of their machines turning fifty spindles was opened in Northampton and operated with some success until it closed in 1764.

The importance of their invention was immortalised, somewhat whimsically, in a poem by John Dyer in 1757:

*A circular machine, of new designIn conic shape: it draws and spins a thread Without the tedious toil of needless hands. A wheel invisible, beneath the floor, To ev'ry member of th' harmonious frame, Gives necessary motion. One intent O'erlooks the work; the carded wool, he says, So smoothly lapped around those cylinders, Which gently turning, yield it to yon cirque Of upright spindles, which with rapid whirl Spin out, in long extent, an even twine.*

Wyatt and Paul's technology was later developed further by Richard Arkwright, who patented his water frame in 1767. It could spin 128 threads at a time. Powered by water, it produced strong, durable thread that was easier to weave into fabric. Interestingly, his patent was later overturned, as the invention was based upon an earlier invention by Thomas Highs from Lancashire.

In 1771 Arkwright installed water frames in his factory on the River Derwent, at Cromford in Derbyshire. As he also used his own carding machines (machines that comb and combine fibres to make them workable via other processes) in the same factory, he created an entirely new concept: a factory that used one continuous process to create a finished product from raw materials under one roof. This was ground breaking in industrial terms. His workers were employed to oversee the machines and worked at specific times – by the clock – rather than during daylight hours as had previously been more the case. He combined water power and machines and was an innovator in employment practices such as shift systems. The machines were in charge now; the workers were there merely to ensure they operated correctly and were kept supplied with the things they needed to operate.

James Hargreaves invented the revolutionary Spinning Jenny – and changed the face of textile production forever – in 1764. According to your point of view at the time, the man was either a genius, who single-handedly revolutionised fabric production – or a devil who stole money out of the pockets of the poor. In the early part of the eighteenth century, many families had earned a living carding and spinning, perhaps as well as farming a few acres. This way of life disappeared with the invention of the Spinning Jenny. In Blackburn, where Hargreaves was based, many members of the working population were employed in the production of 'Blackburn greys' – cloths woven with a linen warp and a cotton weft.

It was not just spinning that was being transformed by new inventions and increasing mechanisation. The textile industry was swiftly becoming mechanised. John Kay patented his flying shuttle in 1773. Kay wove broadloom fabrics and this width required two weavers to sit at the loom, one either side, to send the shuttle backwards and forwards. When the shuttle stopped, it could create imperfections in the weave. Kay invented a system whereby a mechanical attachment controlled by a cord, which could be tugged by the weaver, sent the shuttle flying though the shed. When the cord was tugged in the opposite direction it sent the shuttle back. The invention meant fewer weavers were needed to operate the looms and that there were fewer imperfections in the fabric being woven. This design would lend itself well to increased automation in the years to come.

The invention of the flying shuttle increased the demand for yarn, as weavers could work twice as fast. The flying shuttle had doubled weaving productivity and cotton production could not keep up with this demand. It allowed one person weaving alone to produce much wider fabric than before – but, sadly for the workers, the invention also halved the required workforce. Previously, any broad-loomed fabric required a person either side. In addition to this, before the invention of the flying shuttle, one weaver required four spinners to keep them supplied with yarn. The invention meant that there was a sharp increase in the quantity of yarn required to keep the looms working. The Spinning Jenny could provide this.

The Spinning Jenny was a multi-spooled spinning frame. It was a key development in the industrialisation of yarn production and weaving during the early Industrial Revolution. It could spin eight threads at once to begin with, and this later grew to up to 120 spools as the technology advanced and became more sophisticated.

The machine consisted of a metal frame with spindles at one end. Roving (carded wool that has been drawn out in long shanks ready for spinning) was attached to the frame, passing through two horizontal wooden bars. The spinner would extend the thread with their left hand and spin a wheel with their right hand which would cause the spindles to turn and the thread to be spun. At first, the yarn was not very strong – but Arkwright's water frames would soon change this.

Hargreaves kept his invention a secret for some time but used Spinning Jennies himself to produce yarn. The price of yarn fell and members of the spinning community in Blackburn were so angry with Hargreaves that they broke into his house and smashed his machines. He fled to Nottingham and set up a textile business with his partner Thomas James.

Hargreaves took out a patent in 1770 but his design was already being copied. His invention had changed the face of weaving forever and by the time he died in 1778, over 20,000 Spinning Jennies were being used in Britain. It was used commonly until around 1810 when it was superseded by the spinning mule.

In 1779 Samuel Crompton invented the spinning mule – a hybrid of the Spinning Jenny and the water frame. The first mule had forty-eight spindles and could produce a pound of thread a day – a huge advance in technology. It produced strong, smooth cotton yarn that could be used for warp or weft. It was later used with a variety of other fibres. Crompton could not afford to patent his invention, so he sold his rights to David Dale who went on to secure the patent.

The draw loom, in use in Mediaeval Europe, was now improved upon in France. In the early seventeenth century, a mechanical draw boy replaced the boys who used to sit at the top of the looms. This allowed an assistant to stand beside the loom and control the cords. Subsequently, the loom was further mechanised and the assistant was dispensed with, reducing the margin of human error. This was of prime importance to French weavers who were producing intricately figured silk.

In 1725 Basile Bouchon invented a mechanism that allowed cords to be automatically selected to create a pattern. The selection was programmed by a roll of paper which was perforated to indicate the pattern. The paper pattern passed round a cylinder which was drawn against needles carrying the cords that controlled the warp threads. Ingeniously, when the needles met unperforated paper, they slid past and when they met a perforation, they passed through the hole and stayed in place. Cords thus selected were drawn down by a treadle operated by the foot of a weaving operative.

In 1745 Jacques de Vaucanson further improved the loom. He managed to create a system where no operator or assistant was required to control the cords, with a complex sliding cylinder. This eased the later development of the Jacquard attachment. Joseph-Marie Jacquard was commissioned to overhaul Vaucanson's loom and in 1801, at the Paris Industrial Exhibition, he demonstrated his improved draw loom. In 1804 he introduced his attachment which was a ground-breaking technological advancement. The attachment was mounted on the top of a loom and operated by a weaver using a treadle. It controlled the creation of patterns via a perforated card, which controlled hooks, with each card representing one throw of the shuttle. Although each Jacquard attachment was limited in so far as the number of hooks it could control (and thus limiting the size of a repeat pattern), several attachments could be used at once. This meant that the weaver could create highly complex patterns with a large repeat and could also weave large pictures.

There were still companies that employed groups of skilled hand weavers at this time, despite the move to factory-based spinning and weaving. William Wilson and Son of Bannockburn in Scotland was a famous producer of high-quality tartan fabric throughout the eighteenth and later into the nineteenth century. They created tartan for the military market as well as for the fashion industry. In the 1780s the company both employed outworkers, who wove in their own homes, and weavers who worked the looms in premises near Stirling. These weavers were provided with their own accommodation, which was purpose built. Eventually, as their business grew, they built a water-powered mill on the banks of the Bannock Burn. It was a large, three-storey building with big windows to let in the all-important light for weaving.

All of these changes created unrest. The Luddite movement formed in Nottingham and grew into a regional rebellion that lasted from 1811 to 1816. It was made up of textile workers who feared for their livelihood with the coming of mechanisation and industrialisation. The group protested that machinery was putting them out of work and eroding any protection they had earned as a result of being part of a skilled labour force. They were afraid that they were being superseded – and rightly so. Their protests became increasingly violent and they smashed machinery as a part of their resistance. The force of the authorities came down upon them harshly and mill owners hired forces to protect them. This resulted in the shooting of protestors. Eventually, the rebellion was crushed by military force.

Johanna Schopenhauer, a German author, described Manchester in 1830:

*Dark and smoky from coal vapours, it resembles a huge forge or workshop. Work, profit and greed seem to be the only thoughts here. The clatter of the cotton mills and the looms can be heard everywhere…*

There were even Georgian weaver poets. Born in 1774, Robert Tannahill 'The Weaver Poet', was a talented writer and lyricist who worked in the textile mills that made Paisley famous. He made himself a makeshift desk that he attached to his loom, where he could write as he wove. He was shy and quiet and liked to walk in the countryside that inspired many of his poems and songs, such as *The Braes O' Gleniffer* and *Gloomy Winters No Awa'*. His poems have been compared to those written by Robert Burns, with common themes including brotherhood, love and the life of the common man.

In 1807 his first collection of poems was published to great success with the aid of subscriptions to fund them. In 1810 he attempted a second collection, without the aid of subscription funding, and publishers refused him. At this point, his friends became worried about his mental state. They tried not to leave him alone for too long as they were worried for his safety.

On 18 May 1810 Tannahill wandered off without telling his family where he was heading. When they noticed that he was missing, a search was held. It was too late for poor Tannahill, who in a depressed state had drowned himself in the canal close to his home. He was buried in the cemetery at Castlehead Kirk, where his grave can be visited today.

I hope he would be comforted to hear that his work is still in print today and is performed regularly, including by the group The Tannahill Weavers who tour the world performing his songs. Paisley still remembers its tragic, poetic son with a statue at the entrance of Abbey Close.

So, the Georgian Era saw expansion in the textile trade at a previously unprecedented level. Technological advances and the introduction of mass factory-scale production changed the face of spinning and weaving for good. Invention followed invention and production of fabric became faster and more efficient. Increasing mechanisation changed the world for textile workers, too, with fewer skilled workers needed as machines were developed to do the work done previously by teams of spinners and weavers. As factories grew and mills were built, the situation worsened for much of the workforce as they were increasingly de-skilled and forced into unpleasant working conditions in a drive for profit and expansion. Unfortunately, worse was yet to come as the Victorian Era ushered in dark times indeed for working people.

*Chapter 8*

# Victorian Spinning and Weaving 1837–1901

The Victorian era saw a further boom in the textiles industry. In parts of the country textiles were the main source of employment for local people. By 1853 there were an astounding 108 cotton mills in Manchester. Cotton mills began opening in towns nearby, such as Oldham and Bury. At its height of production, Oldham was the most productive cotton spinning town globally.

The Bridgewater Canal ran like an artery into Manchester bringing raw cotton from the West Indies and the southern states of America, through the docks at Liverpool and thus to the factories to be spun. The growing railway network created links that the burgeoning textiles industry used to move goods and materials between Manchester and the surrounding mill towns. Before these innovations, raw materials and fabrics had all been moved slowly on pack horses, along bridleways.

Mills sprang up in Blackburn, Rochdale, Burnley and Bolton – referred to as 'Spindleton' in 1892. As the mills migrated from the centre of Manchester to these surrounding towns, the commercial centre of the town grew. Warehouses, services and the all-important banks to finance the trade grew up around the Royal Exchange. The first exchange was built on the site in 1727, but it was rebuilt several times, with each incarnation grander than the previous one. Queen Victoria visited in 1851 and granted the title of 'Royal Exchange'.

In the 1870s the term 'Cottonopolis' entered popular parlance, such was the importance of the cotton trade. Many of the magnificent buildings in the centre of Manchester were built as a result of this lucrative trade. But what were conditions like in the factories for the workers?

Political scientist and historian Alexis de Tocqueville described Manchester in sombre terms in the 1830s:

> *A thick black smoke covers the city. The sun appears like a disc without any rays. In this semi-daylight 300,000 people work ceaselessly. A thousand noises rise amidst this unending damp and dark labyrinth... the footsteps of a busy crowd, the crunching wheels of machines, the shriek of steam from the boilers, the regular beat of looms...*
>
> *Oeuvres Complètes* (1835)

Leeds was also a major centre for the textile industry in the Victorian period. It had been a cloth-making town since the sixteenth century and was in the vanguard of the Industrial Revolution. It grew further as transport links improved in the Victorian era. Wool was shipped to Leeds from across the empire – from as far away as New Zealand and Australia. The Leeds textile mills continued to prosper well into the twentieth century and only declined as cheap Far Eastern fabric imports poured into England in the 1960s.

Wool production was still so lucrative that terrible actions were carried out to increase profits for landowners. In Wales and Scotland smallholders and crofters were driven from their land as greedy landowners switched from arable to sheep-grazing land. The Highland Clearances that had begun back in the 1750s continued for a century. Tenants were brutally evicted from the land they tilled – sometimes land that had been held by the same families for generations. The crofts were destroyed by the drive for profit and cottages were knocked down. Terrible hardship followed, with whole communities being obliterated as famine and death stalked the Highlands. Many people fled the country as emigrants and sailed to the New World to make a new life in Canada and America.

By 1850 there were 260,000 power looms in Britain. The rise of the power loom had led to the reduction in demand for skilled weavers. This caused a reduction in wages and even unemployment for these skilled craftsmen. The power loom also opened up weaving in the factory to women and children as the machinery required less muscle power to operate. It was a noisy, dangerous – and often short – life.

Children were cheap labour. An adult man could earn around fifteen shillings a week; a woman around seven shillings, whilst a child would only earn around three shillings a week. Many factories preferred to employ women and children to save money on wages. The small size of the employed children meant they could do jobs adults could not such as crawl into small spaces to maintain machinery. 'Parish apprentices' were children taken from workhouses and orphanages in the south (where they were living 'on the parish' i.e. being supposedly looked after by the authorities) and 'apprenticed' to factory owners. Supposedly, they would be taught the textile trade, so they could work for a living as they got older and take care of themselves. In reality, these poor children were taken to live in barracks attached to the factories and worked gruelling twelve-hour shifts. The owners would have two shifts, so that as one team finished for the day and went back to the barracks, another would be leaving their beds to begin the day.

Conditions in the mills and factories were appalling. In cotton mills, for example, the air had to be humid and damp for the materials to be spun at optimal efficiency. The air was full of dust and fibre particles, and workers – especially children – would suffer from chest and lung diseases and pneumonia. Tuberculosis was rife and weavers spread it via 'kissing the shuttle' – wetting the thread with their mouths before drawing it through. Where cloth was woven, the looms were cacophonous and workers suffered from hearing loss. Card room workers often contracted byssinosis, a lung disease caused by prolonged inhalation of textile fibre dust, and many mule-spinners contracted cancer of the scrotum, due to the oils being sprayed at crotch level to maintain the smooth operation of the machines as they worked.

Accidents were commonplace; up to 40 per cent of accidents recorded at the Manchester Infirmary in 1833, for example, were factory accidents. Many of those injured were children who were forced to crawl into the body of the machinery, which worked without guards, in order to maintain them. The machines were expensive and the children of the poor were seen as expendable. When the flying shuttle was introduced, it was seen as a breakthrough invention as it speeded up the weaving process exponentially. However, it was dangerous technology, as if the shuttle was deflected from its correct path through the machine, it would shoot out at speed, striking workers in its path. Injury records of the time are full of awful accidents involving flying shuttles, including many instances of workers losing an eye due to malfunction in the machinery. In 1901, after long debates in the House of Commons, machine guards and other safety measures began to be installed in this type of heavy machinery.

Discipline was harsh. Children who 'misbehaved' were hit with leather straps, hung from the roof in baskets and had weights hung around their necks. The poor mites were doused with freezing water to keep them awake if they dozed off.

Eventually, a reform movement began to raise its voice, speaking out against these appalling conditions. A report into factory conditions was written by Michael Sadler in 1832. It included testimonies from factory workers describing their awful working conditions. It included the conditions in factories and mills for children and the public were shocked at the grave situation. This report helped to pave the way for Lord Shaftesbury's campaign for factory reforms that would improve conditions for all. He fought against ignorance and greed and the view that improving conditions would lead to a ruin of industry as new measures ate into profits. Some people, such as economist Adam Smith, even argued that the poor conditions reported from the factories had been exaggerated.

Robert Owen owned a cotton mill in New Lanark, Scotland. He believed that people who were treated well would work harder. He provided decent housing and a school for his workers and their families and did not employ anyone under the age of ten. In 1834 he even took the unprecedented step of setting up a union for his workers, the Grand Consolidated Trades Union, to ensure their needs were met and their rights were respected.

Titus Salt was another reformer involved in the textile industry. The son of a wool stapler, after attending grammar school he joined the family business in 1824. Daniel Salt and Son became one of the most successful textile companies in Bradford. When his father retired, Titus took the helm of the business. Within twenty years he was the biggest employer in Bradford.

Bradford was horribly polluted at this time; the air full of choking smoke and fumes, and the River Beck – where the town's drinking water came from – was full of sewage. Typhoid and Cholera stalked the streets and life expectancy was a frighteningly-short eighteen years. It seems incredible today to think that only a sobering 30 per cent of children born to textile workers reached the age of fifteen.

German writer George Weerth lived in Bradford from 1843 to 1846. He was a companion of Friedrich Engels, whose father owned a large textile factory in Manchester. Weerth wrote extensively about the working class; textile workers in particular as he also worked as a representative of a textiles firm. He wrote:

*Every other factory town in England is a paradise in comparison to this hole. In Manchester the air lies like lead upon you; in Birmingham it*

*is just as if you were sitting with your nose in a stove pipe; in Leeds
you have to cough with the dust and the stink as if you had swallowed
a pound of Cayenne pepper in one go – but you can put up with all
that. In Bradford, however, you think you have been lodged with the
devil incarnate. If anyone wants to feel how a poor sinner is tormented
in Purgatory, let him travel to Bradford.*

Titus Salt owned five mills in Bradford. Although he opposed unionisation
and still employed young children in his factories, Salt worked to improve
conditions for his workers. He found that using the Rodda Smoke Burner
in his mills caused much less pollution and tried to persuade Bradford
Council to make their use mandatory, but other factory owners resisted.
In 1848 he became the mayor of Bradford, but the council still did not
join him in his quest to improve the air – and thus, health of the workers –
in Bradford. Finally, he moved his business out of the town, building an
industrial community in the countryside on the banks of the River Aire,
which he rather pompously named 'Saltaire'. By 1870 the community was
created. The mill was at the centre and at the time was the largest in Europe.
Flues were fitted to clean the air inside the factory and the chimney was
fitted with a Rodda Smoke Burner to maintain clean air outside. Noise
was muffled by putting a lot of the machinery underground. The working
conditions were much better than in most mills of the time.

There were 850 houses for the 3,500 workers employed by Salt, along
with a school, hospital, church, library, public baths, wash houses, shops
and even a park. The houses were supplied with piped, clean water from a
purpose-built reservoir. Gas was piped in to provide lighting and heating.
Houses even had their own outside lavatory.

*Reynolds Weekly Newspaper*, a successful radical paper founded by
George William MacArthur Reynolds in 1850, reported on Saltaire,
saying:

*The site chosen for Saltaire is, in many ways, desirable. The scenery in the immediate neighbourhood is romantic, rural and beautiful. A better looking body of factory 'hands' than those in Saltaire I have not seen. They are far above the average of their class in Lancashire, and are considerably above the majority in Yorkshire.*

When Salt died in 1876, it was estimated that he had given away over £500,000 (£55,948,544.90 equivalent in 2018) over his lifetime to charitable causes.

Just before the turn of the century in 1889, a sense of nostalgia for handloom weaving and a kind of benign social engineering led to the creation of an organisation called The Scottish Home Industries Association. It was felt that home-based handloom weaving should be encouraged and strengthened in rural, and particularly, Highland communities such as the Hebrides, where it was a traditional trade, for the good of the community. The association helped people in the Hebridean community to buy weaving equipment so that they could produce traditional tweed fabric. The association also sent instructors to the islands to help to support weavers with advice.

William Blake's 'dark Satanic Mills' existed in truth. Blake saw the Industrial Revolution as ushering in the destruction of nature and of human relationships, and the cotton mills (as well as the collieries) as a way that millions were enslaved. It must have seemed that way to many of the poor textile workers of the day, who were often beaten and harshly disciplined to keep them in order, even the tiniest children. The Victorian era saw great fortunes made, but it also saw the subjugation of a whole class of people to provide those profits. Accidents were common, mortality was high, and children were used as cheap labour, often not living to reach adulthood. The cities and towns were polluted, and disease ridden. Gorgeous yarn was spun and beautiful fabrics were woven – but at what cost?

## Chapter 9

# Twentieth Century Spinning and Weaving

At the dawning of the twentieth century, the textile trade was a massive employer and source of great wealth in Britain. In 1910 in Blackburn, Lancashire, out of a population of 133,000 an incredible 42,000 were employed in the textile industry; 28,000 of those were weavers, giving Blackburn the highest concentration of weavers in any town in the world. Burnley, not far away, housed 26,000 weavers, with 814 of these being children as young as twelve. Between 1910 and 1911 the number of looms in Blackburn burgeoned from 19,500 to 87,400 – a stunning rate of growth.

Textiles were booming and there were fortunes to be made. Fabulous buildings flew up, funded by the textile wealth. Manchester's Royal Exchange began to be ostentatiously rebuilt at around the time of the First World War and was completed in 1921. Its massive trading hall was nearly 30 metres tall, and there was an imposing central glass dome. It had a membership of 11,000 cotton merchants and traders. It was damaged during The Second World War and ceased cotton trading in 1968.

At its peak, in the early twentieth century, the Lancashire cotton industry alone employed around 6,000 people. It produced eight billion yards of cloth per year by 1912. In 1914, at the outset of the First World War, 78 per cent of cotton produced was exported, mainly to the Far East. In 1913 India imported an almost unimaginable 3,000 million yards of British cotton.

However, the outbreak of the First World War was disastrous for the textile industry as well as a disaster in terms of lives lost. During the war, fabrics could not be exported to foreign markets, and those gaps in the market were filled by other countries. Areas such as Blackburn suffered from massive unemployment.

Some privations led to innovations, however Nettlecloth, woven in the ancient era and still produced and worn by the poor in mediaeval times was produced in great quantities during the First World War. The German army, for example, made uniforms from nettlecloth as there was a shortage of cotton.

The British cotton industry never truly recovered from the changes during and after the First World War, but in northern towns such as Blackburn, the textile industry continued to be a major employer. In 1929, despite the closures, 88.7 per cent of working women over eighteen were employed in the industry and 74.2 per cent in the Burnley area.

Technology continued to develop. In the 1920s the first shuttleless looms appeared. In 1927 a Swiss company called Sulzer Brothers had the exclusive rights to these new, faster looms. Today, Sulzer weaving machines are still used.

In the 1930s the textile industry in Britain slumped. Japan for the first time set up its own cotton factories, which grew into a major industry. It produced cheaper cloth than Britain and by 1933 it had even introduced 24-hour cotton production, radically increasing production and thus becoming the world's largest cotton manufacturer. In addition to this, the move for Indian independence in the 1930s further undermined the British export trade. Ghandi called for a boycott of Lancashire cotton and when this boycott was adhered to it was a killing blow – India accounted for half of Britain's cotton exports. The British cotton market suddenly collapsed and mill owners began to close down operations. Seventy-four cotton mills in Lancashire closed within four years. By the late 1930s exports had fallen to 2,000 million yards.

Artisanal, home-based spinners and weavers still carried on creating cloth during this period. The nostalgia for 'things past' that began with the founding of organisations such as The Scottish Home Industries Association continued in some sort of longing in the public conscience for a bucolic rural idyll that perhaps never existed in truth. Tweed hand weavers, such as those in the Harris Tweed industry for example, were seen as an iconic representation of days of yore.

This excerpt from *The Scotsman* in September 1929 is the epitome of this view, speaking about the death of a tweed weaver from Glenaray:

*LAST OF THE HANDLOOM WEAVERS.*
*Mr Angus Munro, farmer, South Tullich, Glenaray, died on Saturday at the age of 76 years. When a tenant of Auchnagoul township, Inveraray, he carried on business as a handloom weaver, the products of his loom in the nature of brown crotal cloth, being purchased by H.R.H. Princess Louise and other Royal personages, who had the cloth made into garments. Members of the nobility from different places also purchased and wore Auchnagoul crotal. Mr Munro was the last handloom weaver in that district. In 1764 there were eleven handloom weavers at work in the old fishing village of Kenmore, five miles from Inveraray, besides many in Inveraray, Carnus, Clenarty and at other places in the Inveraray district.*

The Second World War brought a slight reprieve for the textile industry, and the Lancashire mills were pressed into service to make textiles for 'the war effort', such as uniforms and parachutes. There were huge profits to be made producing uniforms for the armed forces. Wool fabric in particular was needed for military uniforms. Civilians were encouraged to 'make do and mend' rather than buy new clothes and rationing also had an effect.

Coldharbour Mill in Devon wove specialist wartime products during both world wars. Run by the Fox Brothers, the mill wove puttees, a type of protective leg bandage worn by soldiers. The term comes from a Hindi word for bandage. It was a long thin strip of fabric wound round the lower leg for extra protection. During the First World War, the puttee was a part of the military uniform of the infantry and the cavalry and was eight feet long. It was wound round the leg between the boots and the breeches.

By the Second World War uniforms had changed and the Fox Brothers adapted the design of the puttees accordingly. They were now just two feet long and covered the ankle alone. During the wars, twelve million pairs of puttees were produced at Coldharbour Mill, along with seven million yards of khaki serge which was made into military uniforms. After the war the fabric woven at Coldharbour evolved into hardwearing workwear and suiting.

Woven fabric was even used in the construction of wartime aircraft. Fabric was used to cover the framework of the planes, to increase structural integrity whilst aiding lift and combating drag – important for efficiency and safety. Early aviators such as George Cayley and Otto Lilienthal had used cotton to cover the frames of their manned gliders. Other aircraft used silk and linen. Fabric was often rubberized or coated with sago starch. In 1911 cellulose 'dope' was developed and this a great step forward for the production of fabric that would remain taut once applied to the framework, so that the aircraft did not need repeated recovering.

First World War aviators bravely flew in fabric covered bi-planes. This was obviously incredibly dangerous due to the flammability of the material and the nitrocellulose dope with which the fabric was treated. We have all seen the terrible images of the Hindenburg airship as it burned; the flammability of the fabric and the dope was a contributory factor, as well as the use of hydrogen gas in its flight.

By the Second World War most planes were made from metal, but fabric surfaces were still part of the early Spitfire designs. Hawker Hurricanes also had a fabric covered fuselage and, until 1939, fabric-covered wings. The de Havilland DH.98 Mosquito, a high speed, high altitude aircraft, had a plywood frame and was covered in 'Madapolam', a soft cotton and linen fabric woven from fine yarns. The equal warp and weft meant that the fabric had great tensile strength.

An incredible story of bravery and ingenuity comes from one of the greatest escape attempt stories in history – from Oflag IV-C, or Colditz Castle. Following the execution of fifty prisoners after The Great Escape from Stalag Luft III in 1944, Allied Command discouraged escape attempts. However, at Colditz Castle, British prisoners cleverly made a glider to attempt to escape, using prison sleeping bags as covering for the frame and home-made glue and dope from boiled millet. The *Colditz Cock* glider never flew, as the prisoners who built her were liberated in April 1945 as the aircraft approached completion. In 2012, however, Tony Hoskins built a full-sized radio-controlled replica of the *Colditz Cock*, which he flew successfully from Colditz for a Channel 4 documentary. Hoskins wrote a book telling the story of the original prisoners, as well as the story of making his replica called *Flight from Colditz*, which was published by Pen and Sword Books in 2016.

During the post-war period there were many advances in textiles as a result of technological research and new yarns were created in the laboratory. Materials like nylon and acrylic were developed, for example. Artificial silk had been available for a long time, since the nineteenth century in the form of rayon, but it was not until the 1940s that nylon was introduced. Women clamoured for the new material, particularly in the form of 'nylons' – shimmering, silky sheer stockings. The creation of synthetic materials became a race to produce the next lucrative innovation. The American company DuPont was a forerunner. In the 1950s, they created artificial wool, called acrylic and in the late 1950s they created spandex, a rubberised material.

In the 1960s the introduction of synthetic fibres, as well as competition from overseas companies employing cheap labour, meant that the wool textile industry went into decline. However, the booming housing market meant there was a sharp increase in the need for carpets to be woven and wool was the primary source of yarn for this. A number of woollen mills left their traditional markets and concentrated fully on the carpet trade.

In the 1950s and 1960s, there was a massive injection of labour into the textile industry via the immigration of workers from the Indian subcontinent. This increased workforce and its cheap labour allowed owners to create a third shift so that the mills were never silent. The Cotton Industry Act in 1959 tried to address problems, looking at modernization and amalgamation of businesses, but it was in vain. Lancashire's textile industry was not competitive in the new international market and it failed. During the 1970s mills in Lancashire shut at a terrifying rate of one mill per week. By the 1980s the industry had all but vanished and the mills were demolished or turned into luxury housing and apartments.

In the 1970s technology enabled weaving to be entirely mechanised and all of the actions of the loom took place simultaneously. These multiphase looms came in two different types: wave shed looms and parallel shedding looms. Multiphase looms are still in use, with the fastest of them producing a stunning 1.5 yards of fabric per minute – something weavers of the past could only dream about.

By the 1980s computer-aided design and manufacture was possible. This dramatically shortened the design process which could be as little as 24 hours, as opposed to the previous situation where design took weeks, or even months to do. Computer designs have the added advantage in the modern day that they can be transmitted digitally to anywhere in the world – much quicker than sending out samples via the postage system. This also reduces costs and means changes can be made without the need to set up a loom or to weave a single line. Computers can control the weaving process, detect and correct mistakes, and work quickly and efficiently.

The twentieth century had been a time of tumultuous change for the textile industry. The century opened with spinning and weaving in the textile factory at an incredible level of production and it was a major employer, particularly in the north of England. Many advances were made technologically, especially in the inter-war and post-war periods with the advent of artificial fibres such as nylon, acrylic and spandex. However, the halt in the export trade during the First World War had dealt the industry a huge blow from which it never truly recovered to its heady turn-of-the-century days. The 1930s brought a further blow in the reduction in trade to India as the country fought for its independence. In this period, England became unable to compete on the international market. By the 1970s, mills were closing in massive numbers, never to reopen. Computer-aided design from the 1980s onwards further mechanised the industry and reduced the need for skilled workers. So what would the twenty-first century bring?

*Chapter 10*

# Modern Spinning and Weaving

Today, in modern mills, fibre is processed mechanically. Cotton and wool are cleaned to remove debris such as burrs, vegetable matter and twigs. Wool is washed to remove dirt and grease (lanolin) and silk fibres are washed to remove sericin, a type of gum that occurs naturally in the cocoons. Fibres are blended to create a uniform mix to create yarn of a consistent quality. Wool, silk and cotton are carded – combed on sheets of needles to separate individual fibres and make them lie in the same direction. This process also removes the smallest of impurities. Fibres used to create fine yarn can also be combed at this stage. Carding industrially produces a thin sheet which is condensed to form a sliver, which can be loosely twisted together to form long shanks called roving.

Modern industrial looms are automated and powered by an electric motor. There are 'flat looms' that produce a continuous sheet of fabric and 'circular looms' that produce tubular fabric. Among flat looms there is a further division. There are so-called 'shuttleless' looms that draw the weft thread from a stationary supply, and shuttle looms. Shuttle looms are divided into a further two categories, according to whether the shuttle is fed thread by an operator, or automatically.

Apart from general engineering refinements, increasing automation and the addition of sensors, modern loom designs are similar to late nineteenth-century looms, and would probably be recognised as such by Victorian weavers, should they have had the opportunity to see one. Textile factories are still noisy places – perhaps noisier than ever, due to the high speed of the operations and the weight of modern shuttles. Noise levels in textile mills are generally above the level where deafness occurs and protective measures are taken to protect operatives. Most recent research into loom design has concentrated on shuttleless technology, as these can reach high speeds and high levels of efficiency with less noise, vibration and wear. All of these technological advances have drastically reduced the need for skilled spinners and weavers in industrial textile production settings.

There are still vestiges of the old traditional weaving businesses, however. Perhaps the best known are the three remaining Scottish Harris Tweed producers in the Outer Hebrides. Harris Tweed has been hand-woven in their homes by islanders from Uist, Harris, Lewis and Barra for centuries. The wool is grown on sheep that graze the islands and dyed and spun traditionally without ever leaving the place where the sheep roam.

Perhaps the most exciting developments in modern spinning and weaving, however, is at an artisanal level. The 'slow' craft movement in particular is embracing and valuing yarn processed by hand, mindfully and in ecologically sound ways. More people than ever are processing, spinning and weaving their own yarn, building upon the techniques of the past; experimenting with new (and ancient, mainly forgotten) fibres. Even at a commercial level, companies are embracing traditional and underused textiles; in Germany, Austria and Italy they have started to produce commercial nettle textiles, for example. People are keeping small, rare breed flocks specifically for their fleeces, and are combining natural and artificial fibres in new and exciting ways. Creative people are mixing fibres, carding wool and spinning away with drop spindles and spinning wheels around the globe. They are adding a rich tapestry of colours, textures and fibres to create art batts (sumptuous mixtures of different colours and textures) and spinning it into art yarn to be woven, felted, knitted or crocheted.

In this modern era the new wave of artisans is once again creating high quality, top grade handmade yarns and woven fabric. This is then made into 'wearable art', sold via websites, at fairs and via blogs and on social media around the world. And indeed, the world has shrunk in the internet age, as artisans learn from one another online, sharing their skills and techniques with great generosity via streaming sites such as YouTube. Weaving and spinning groups abound on social media, with artisans collaborating with one another, sharing their skills and techniques and offering a whole new world market of fibre and equipment supplies.

There is a renaissance in fibre arts and it is primarily driven by small, micro producers of yarn and woven fabric at an artisanal level. The growth in spinning and weaving guilds, as well as the burgeoning of wool and fibre festivals is testament to the increase in popularity these ancient crafts are currently enjoying. It has never been easier to discover a new craft, or to learn how to achieve good results, or to buy the supplies needed for spinning and weaving, with access to fibre from around the globe at the click of a computer mouse. Online and distance courses are available, so that wherever you are in the world, you can get started on your journey to becoming a spinner or weaver.

**Why spin and weave yourself?**

The contemplative nature of spinning and weaving offers a balm in a busy world. It allows the crafter to step outside their stresses and worries and concentrate only on colour, texture and the creation of beautiful artefacts and clothing.

Spinning with a drop spindle or on a spinning wheel allows you to make exactly the yarn you desire – the colour, texture and weight. You decide what to include and what to leave out. You can experiment with different fibres, from merino and silk, to alpaca, cotton, flax, hemp, nettle, soya and rose fibre. You can create beautiful colourways and mixes that nobody else can. You can control the quality of your yarn and will enjoy even more weaving, knitting or crocheting with the results.

You can even decide to take a fleece, sheered straight from the animal, and process the whole thing. You can skirt it yourself (remove vegetable matter such as straw etc), wash the fleece gently and watch it dry in the sun in the same way as hundreds of generations before you have done. You can then card your wool on hand carders, a blending board or on a hand-cranked (or electric) carding machine, and blend it with other fibres, both natural and artificial. The sense of achievement when you do this is phenomenal. The fibre can then be spun and woven into fabric.

It is very grounding to carry out these actions, knowing that you are doing something that has been done for tens of thousands of years. Spinning itself can also be a highly social pastime. There are many guilds around the world that you can join to help you along the road and develop your skills and it is a great way to meet like-minded crafters and artisans. They often hold courses and demonstrations. Feeling part of an artistic yarn community is both supportive and satisfying. Should you decide to buy a spinning wheel, you will find they are relatively easy to run and maintain. You can even buy travel wheels that fit into a holdall to carry around with you to different locations and meets.

Read through the artisan interviews that follow to find out more about the world of spinning and weaving today.

## Chapter 11

# Artisan Interviews

The best way to find out about the modern artisans working in spinning and weaving today is to ask them about their experiences, inspirations and artistic practices. With the advent of the internet, it is easier than ever to find a window into the creative world of these artisans and to find out more.

These artists and crafters earn a living with their craft. They have taken the leap into self-employment and sustain themselves and their families with their skill and artistry. I asked the artists a series of questions and encouraged them to describe their motivations, inspirations and goals for the future. They have taken traditional techniques and allowed them to evolve as they have explored their own ways of working.

You can find out more about each artist by following the links provided for their websites and social media. You can also buy their products directly, or even commission pieces yourself, and help to support the hand-made industry directly at source!

### Sharon Poole, Weaver, Somerset UK

*What first attracted you to your craft?*

In one word – colour. Present me with a pile of fabric or yarns and it is like putting a small child in a sweet shop! I have been attracted to fibre arts and crafts since childhood. Growing up in the 1960s, my mother made many of my clothes and I was always given the remnants to make dolls' clothes with. I also made a patchwork quilt with my mother, sewing tiny squares of cotton fabric over papers in the old-fashioned way, before

Gorgeous hand-spun and knitted cowl by Sharon Poole.

assembling the whole. My attraction to weaving lies in the combination of colour and texture, combined with the basic simplicity of the craft. With a loom and yarn, there are infinite possibilities.

*Can you describe your journey into your craft? How did you get started? For example, do you have particular training or qualifications, or are you self-taught?* Over the years I have done dressmaking, knitting, patchwork, quilting, spinning and weaving. In the main I am self-taught but have attended classes on specific techniques. In the early 1990s I spotted a Patchwork & Quilting magazine in a shop and was entranced by the wonderful modern fabrics then becoming available. The old image of floral, pastel designs was being replaced by vibrant geometric and ombre fabrics by designers such as Nancy Crow and Jinny Beyer. For the next 15 years or so, most

Sharon Poole's glorious work is inspired by the landscape around her. Her creativity is fired by her travels, especially landscapes and seascapes. She loves the Scottish Highlands – soft greys, purples and pale blue with mossy greens – and the thermal areas of New Zealand – greys and muddy colours contrasting with vivid lime greens and yellows of lichens.

Gilleoin Finlay-Coull's vibrant bluebell wood freeform cushion inspired by the natural world.

*Above left*: Carol Gascoigne's beautifully woven alpaca shawl

*Above right*: Carol Gascoigne's process of weaving a subtly toned scarf in shades of blue and grey

Sharon Poole's cotton wrap is a cascade of colour.

Gorgeous shade of green yarn created by Gilleoin Finlay-Coull

Gilleoin Finlay-Coull's lovely felted picture of the highlands of Scotland, created with fibre

Pauline Campbell's lovely hand dyed yarn 'Mapper.' Pauline chooses the names of her yarns after a theme based on Victoriana. She attaches a story to them, she says, 'so that when people are knitting with the yarn, they are taken on a journey through the different tones and shades.'

*Above left*: Beautiful notebook cover created from felted fibres by Ffibrau Y Gwyr – Fibres of Gower

*Above right*: Lilac crocheted hat from Ffibrau Y Gwyr – Fibres of Gower

*Above left*: Beautiful soft shawl woven by Sharon Poole

*Above right*: Vibrantly dyed yarn scarf woven by Sharon Poole

Glorious natural shades of broom and heather created by Sharon Poole.

*Above left*: Sharon Poole's natural shades of broom and heather woven into a timeless shawl.

*Above right*: Fabulous fluorite shades of yarn created by Pauline Campbell, named 'Steampunk Dragonfly.'

Rich, earthy shades of yarn created by Pauline Campbell, named 'The Alchemist'.

*Above*: Beautiful woven piece from Ffibrau Y Gwyr – Fibres of Gower

*Right*: Plait of beautifully dyed wool in natural shades from Ffibrau Y Gwyr – Fibres of Gower

Lovely spun yarn from Ffibrau Y Gwyr – Fibres of Gower

Freshly carded batts of wool from Ffibrau Y Gwyr – Fibres of Gower

Spring shades of fibre from Ffibrau Y Gwyr – Fibres of Gower

of my spare time (I then had a full-time career as a social history curator in a museum together with increasing caring responsibilities) was spent designing, cutting and sewing quilts and wall-hangings. In 1997 I won first prizes in the Theme category 'Across the Atlantic' at *Quilts UK* and *Popular Patchwork* magazine's Miniature Quilt competition. I also had a large wall-hanging juried into the Tactile Architecture category in the largest quilt exhibition in the world at Houston, Texas in 2000.

Whilst I love to create, I also prefer the end results to have purpose and slowly I was losing my passion for patchwork. Since 2003 I have been lucky enough to reduce my working hours and indulge myself in travel and photography (another long-standing interest). In Guatemala and Bali I watched local women weaving. The bright colours and rhythmic motions of the craft immediately sparked an interest I wanted to explore further. This came at the perfect time for me as I planned to retire from paid employment at the end of 2017 and weaving could not only stimulate my mind but hopefully provide an income, however small, as well.

*Do you have any inspirations or influences? This could include particular artisans, periods in history etc.*
My main influences come from my travels, especially landscapes and seascapes. I was particularly inspired by the colours of the Scottish Highlands – soft greys, purples and pale blue with mossy greens – and the thermal areas of New Zealand – greys and muddy colours contrasting with vivid lime greens and yellows of lichens.

*What do you enjoy most about working with the materials that you choose to work with?*
I love that I am using natural fibres – cotton, silk and wool. I have also been experimenting with recycled sari silk, made by a women's collective in the Himalayas.

*Please describe the tools of your craft and how you use them.*

I now have four looms – a 24-inch rigid heddle loom, two folding rigid heddle looms of 16 and 20 inches, which I can take with me when travelling or to shows, and a four-shaft table loom. I particularly enjoy making long wraps and shawls. I still have much to learn about what these basically simple looms can achieve.

*Describe your business. What items do you make? Do you sell items – if so, what? Do you teach courses? Describe the thing you have made that has made you most proud.*

My business is in its infancy still but I was very pleased to receive my first commission – a multi-coloured cotton gamp wrap to be given to the commissioner's sister as a milestone birthday gift.

*Please describe a typical day.*

My head often overflows with ideas, so I have to jot notes down constantly, but I don't really have a typical day. I would expect to spend anything between one and three hours weaving.

*What traditional 'heritage' methods do you use in your craft?*

Plain weave is as old as cloth. Loom weights made in the Iron Age have been found on the hillside where I live in Somerset. Most of my wraps are produced in plain or balanced weave, to showcase the colour of the natural yarns I use.

*How have you adapted heritage or historic methods for the modern day?*

Beyond using modern versions of old looms, no adaptation is required.

*What advice would you give someone starting out in your field?*

Join a local Guild of Weavers, Spinners and Dyers for the wonderful peer support and sharing of knowledge they offer. Many guilds also own equipment for loan. Then read, read and read.

**About me:**

After school, I attended an Art Foundation Course covering painting, print-making, textile printing and photography, before taking a job as a curatorial assistant in a museum. Over the years I eventually became a Social History Officer, looking after the social and local history collections of North Somerset Museum Service. This afforded me access to period costume and craft tools and I loved preparing displays and exhibitions, sometimes using period knitting patterns etc to produce replica garments.

The role also gave me the opportunity to start my writing career which continues to this day, mainly on local history but also now on maritime subjects. Now retired, my love of travel and photography feeds my passions for weaving and other fibre arts and I may come home with hundreds of photos of inspiration!

**Ffibrau Y Gwyr – Fibres of Gower**

Tasha Middleton of Sew Swansea fame, a local and talented textile artist and Rachel Broughton a local fibre artist and all-round textile enthusiast.

*What first attracted you to your craft?*

RACHEL: I have a passion for textiles generally and I love to share that passion with others. I live in an area of the country with a rich textile history and so I really wanted to combine the two by offering courses and kits to introduce textiles and heritage crafts to others. We operate from a recreated historic woollen mill at the Gower Heritage Centre which is the perfect place to introduce others to our local heritage generally as well as to its textiles.

TASHA: I've been creative for as long as I remember. My love of textiles probably started when I was about 17, first of all with drapery and

Glorious wool hand dyed and then spun from Ffibrau Y Gwyr – Fibres of Gower.

dressmaking but as I discovered more crafts and art forms, I fell in love with them and wanted to learn more and more.

*Can you describe your journey into your craft? How did you get started? For example, do you have particular training or qualifications, or are you self-taught?*
RACHEL: I am primarily a self-taught enthusiast with many years experience of textile and woollen crafts. I developed my love for textiles whilst still at school and have come back to it now by developing Ffibrau Y Gwyr. I am hoping my journey will lead me to creating a business

that is sustainable going forward. The use of the Gower Heritage Centre Woollen Mill allowed us the appropriate opportunity to diversify our skills and together offer workshops and kits in a wide range of heritage crafts. The combination of the two means that we have the background of learning new skills for ourselves as well as teaching them.

TASHA: I became pregnant at 17; it was a lonely and isolating experience and to keep myself busy and occupied I started making things. I'd not enjoyed textiles at school but found this desire to work with fabrics that I'd never had before. I taught myself to sew, drape and screen print at home, when I got to a point where I needed to know more I began studying Fashion Design and Textiles in Sussex. I got the chance to learn about not only sewing and fashion design but printing, dyeing and machine knitting. After this I continued experimenting and learning and became self-employed selling products and designs across the country.

After moving to Wales in 2013 I continued sewing, but for various companies until 2016 when I set up Sew Swansea where I teach sewing, dressmaking and textile arts from my city-centre studio. It was through this that I was offered the Gower Heritage Centre Woollen Mill and I approached Rachel, knowing her passion for fibre arts, about setting up a new business focusing on heritage crafts.

Rachel is the perfect partner for this project as her enthusiasm comes through in everything she does. We are very well matched in terms of love of textile arts and can offer such a vast range of skills between us.

*Do you have any inspirations or influences? This could include particular artisans, periods in history etc.*
The Dobcross loom in the Heritage Centre Woollen Mill dates from the early 1900s and originates from one of the last functioning woollen mills in the Swansea area. Our woollen mill is a recreation of an original mill near the site that dated from around 1810 and therefore we focus

our inspiration around this time. The local mill produced a distinctive pattern known as the Gower Minka and we are keen to research further the role this design played in the local textile industry.

Aside from this, our inspiration comes from our environment. Gower was the UK's first area of outstanding natural beauty and therefore we attempt to anchor the workshops and kits we offer to the local environment whether that be in the materials we use, the colour inspiration or local landmarks.

TASHA: Swansea is full of amazing people – so artistic and creative. It's been amazing meeting so many wonderful people, both students and other artists through our work. It's these connections and the building of relationships that encourage me the most, I think, that and the beauty of South Wales; there is no denying it's stunning here and it plays a huge part in influencing the work we do.

*What do you enjoy most about working with the materials that you choose to work with?*

RACHEL: The scope and variety of artistic techniques associated with textiles, and most often wool, is what is most enjoyable. We offer workshops in a range of weaving techniques as well as dyeing workshops working with commercially spun yarn and fibre. We process raw fleece and see that material through to the finished items. There is little better than seeing a fleece running about the field on the back of a sheep before it is then made into a beautiful jumper to be treasured. It is the joy of using locally sourced fibres and creating items for display as well as teaching others to appreciate the materials around them and the opportunities they afford.

Plastic waste is very much on the agenda in Gower and we are keen to link our heritage workshops to an emphasis on making your own, using natural materials and avoiding, where possible, the use of materials that contribute to plastic waste and waste generally.

A handmade item, particularly an item of clothing, is treasured and leads to an appreciation of the effort it takes to create them. Such items are not then thrown away in the way that commercially produced clothing can so often be.

TASHA: As Rachel has said, it really is the range of things that you can do with fibre and yarn that makes them such amazing things to work with. Each technique creates such a different feeling and then combining

Finely woven *mug rug* from Ffibrau Y Gwyr – Fibres of Gower.

everything from dyeing, to spinning, to weaving and it's like magic. The whole process is incredible.

*Please describe the tools of your craft, and how you use them.*
RACHEL: We use a number of different types of loom including rigid heddle looms, inkle looms for tablet weaving, floor looms and the Dobcross Victorian mechanised loom. We work with all types of natural fibres from animal products to plant-based fibres. We spin using hand spindles and spinning wheels as well as knit and crochet finished items.

*Describe your business. What items do you make? Do you sell items – if so, what? Do you teach courses? Describe the thing you have made that has made you most proud.*
RACHEL: Ffibrau Y Gwyr or Fibres of the Gower is a not-for-profit social enterprise partnership. We aim to educate, demonstrate and share our passion for heritage crafts and Welsh manufacturing. We operate from Parkmill, the fantastic, recreated woollen mill at the heart of the Gower Heritage Centre on the Gower Peninsula, close to the city of Swansea.

The Heritage Centre has recreated John Grant's Woollen Mill dating from 1816. It is equipped with a truly awesome and fully functioning Dobcross Loom. We are also equipped with an array of floor looms, handlooms, as well as processing, carding, spinning and dyeing equipment.

Whilst not professing to be history 'buffs' we have found the opportunity hugely exciting, in part due to the layers of local history about the area and its mills to be peeled back one fibre at a time, and of course for the opportunity to develop and teach traditional, heritage crafts whilst recreating a range of traditional Gower woven cloths and bedspreads. We hope to offer a refreshing range of opportunities for those who share our passion.

Someone once called us 'Fibre Freaks' and, well....to be honest they were absolutely right! We love all things fibre and textile related and so, for us, being offered the opportunity to develop textiles from sheep to finished product within our home area is just superb. Keeping our local traditions alive is so important as technology moves us forward at such an astounding rate doesn't it?

We are looking forward to a long and exciting journey as we wrap ourselves in textiles from the felted to the handwoven to the machine woven and knitted...in a riot of inspiring colour as we explore natural dyeing techniques to create a range of naturally dyed yarn.

We are huge believers in the good that crafting can do for self-confidence, well-being and self-esteem, all hugely important in our busy modern lives. Combining a little self-care with some new crafting experience can lift the spirits no end and with our mill nestled in a beautiful valley close to Three Cliffs Bay, one of Gower's most stunning beaches, a visit could offer much more than you think. It certainly did for us!

We offer a range of workshops and experiences in weaving, felt making, rug making, yarn and fibre dyeing as well as spinning, crochet and knitting.

We aim to attract experienced crafters and those who fancy learning a new skill and learning something of the local textile industry. Equally visitors can attend the mill and look at the history.

Our objectives are:

1. To raise awareness of the history of the local woollen industry in Swansea/Gower.
2. To research and recreate heritage weaving patterns associated with Swansea/Gower.
3. To reproduce historic woven cloths from locally sourced materials and market it outside the community, thereby raising awareness of the once lost local industry more widely across the UK and beyond.

4. To develop heritage craft skills and pass them on via the conduct of workshops and teaching.
5. To maintain and develop a working weaving workshop at Gower Heritage Centre for the purposes of furthering our mission.
6. To use textiles to raise awareness of issues in the local community, using crafts in activism to raise that awareness.
7. To source materials locally to produce textile products with local providence thereby renewing, in part, the local textile economy which declined in the early 1800s.

The partnership's vision is to develop an operational woollen mill creating bespoke fabrics for sale whilst also interacting with visitors and offering a wide range of classes in heritage crafts.

Beautifully textured Shetland wool, spun on a spindle from Ffibrau Y Gwyr – Fibres of Gower. The wool creates a buttery blend of textured yarn.

We are most proud of our ability to teach these skills to others because it raises awareness of the local history whilst introducing others to new skills that they can then develop and pass on. There is little better than seeing attendees leave a workshop enthused with the new skills they have acquired and eager to try others.

*Please describe a typical day.*
RACHEL: We are keen to ensure that our workshops are accessible to everyone, even the majority of us who have work commitments during the working week. As a result, most of our workshops take place at evenings and weekends. We spend our time developing our workshops and creating kits to spread the joy associated with the textile industry. We have kits in weaving and dyeing. We offer yarn and fibre for sale as well as felted notebook kits.

A typical workshop sees all materials provided so that attendees need only bring themselves. We believe this is important so that people feel they can give new skills a go without heavy investment. We plan our classes so that we can teach people in small groups and ensure that they get the most from the experience.

We plan market stalls and craft fairs and marketing initiatives to get the word out about the services we offer.

*What traditional 'heritage' methods do you use in your craft?*
RACHEL: Weaving, spinning, felting, dyeing, crochet, knitting. Weaving includes a range of techniques using rigid heddle looms, creative weaving on small frames and tablet weaving. Spinning on drop spindles is a particularly ancient heritage spinning method and yet hugely rewarding and simple. We also look for local artisans to come in and offer courses in other local crafts including welsh basket making.

*How have you adapted heritage or historic methods for the modern day?*
RACHEL: The methods remain virtually unaltered. The only changes we have made are to the ensure that our workshops are accessible in the times and locations they are offered and that they offer a relaxed environment to encourage creativity. They are entirely non-judgmental and we simply want people to enjoy giving these techniques a try. We want our workshops to be socially engaging and enjoyable as the modern world now recognises the benefits of crafting and creativity to well-being and mental health.

Occasionally we use modern materials in traditional weaving where they offer beginners ease of use; acrylic yarn is occasionally used in beginners' weaving for example.

We have access to a greater range of fibres than historic weavers and spinners may have had, but we still obtain fleece locally as our primary source of material. Local produce and traceability are important to us and would have been a given in historic times.

*What advice would you give someone starting out in your field?*
RACHEL: It takes a lot of time and effort both as regards the crafts as well as the marketing! Social media is a great help and is the one major way these businesses obviously differ from times gone by!

The biggest challenge is getting word out about the services we offer as traditional advertising can be expensive. It is essential to think outside the box and be creative on that front as well as with the textiles. Feedback is important so we always ask our attendees to tell us honestly what they think and how we could improve. Be prepared to put in time, have patience and work hard!

TASHA: I'd say stay true to yourself, your vision for your business and work as hard as you can. Your passion for what you do shines through and that attracts people. If you lose that by trying to be commercial or fit in you won't be happy and self-happiness is the key. I'd also say, never stop learning. You can never ever know too much.

Website: *www.ffibrauygwyr.co.uk*

Facebook – *Ffibrau Y Gwyr*

Instagram – *ffibrau_y_gwyr*

Twitter – @ffibrauygwyr

## Venus Bay Eco Retreat, Victoria, Australia

*What first attracted you to your craft?*

Craft practice has always been an element of my creative visual arts practice. I am currently working with Fibre Art as an extension of painting, drawing and relief sculpture.

*Can you describe your journey into your craft? How did you get started? For example, do you have particular training or qualifications, or are you self-taught?*

I have Bachelor Degrees in Fine Art and Arts Education, with 15+ years of experience in arts administration and as a practising contemporary visual artist. I began working with Fibre Art three years ago. Fibre art is a new medium for me derived from my experiences in nature conservation, and my search for a nature based and sustainable medium for personal expression.

*Do you have any inspirations or influences? This could include particular artisans, periods in history etc.*

Yes, I am inspired by indigenous weaving from all over the world, and by current contemporary artists who are challenging the concept that fibre art is simply craft. I like conceptual work that seeks to draw out the less obvious or subliminal elements of art practice. I am particularly interested in women artists and how they are successfully challenging the preconceived and entrenched notion that women's craft work is less relevant or inferior within the context of contemporary fine art practice.

*What do you enjoy most about working with the materials that you choose to work with?*
The connection to country as I use mostly local indigenous plants, the accessibility and low toxicity of the materials, the strong connection to tradition and ancient cultures.

*Please describe the tools of your craft, and how you use them.*
I use very simple tools that are used for embroidery, sewing and basketry. My techniques are simple. I work on my bushland property which is managed under a Trust for Nature conservation covenant and integrate fibre art making into the daily routine of looking after the land.

*Describe your business. What items do you make? Do you sell items – if so, what? Do you teach courses? Describe the thing you have made that has made you most proud.*
I do all the above. I held my first solo exhibition of Fibre Art in 2017 and this was a challenging but worthwhile experience. I have sold most of the work I have made so far including functional baskets and conceptual wall-mounted works. I intend to keep developing and refining my art practice and will be teaching my first two-day fibre art workshop one week from today. The workshop is called 'Creative Custodians – listening to the wild song of our land'.

*Please describe a typical day.*
I rise early and eat a wholefood breakfast. I light the slow combustion wood-heater in the centre of my studio (in winter) and then work on the

computer for up to two hours. I work outside in the bushland, planting trees, removing weeds, stacking wood etc and also maintain a vegetable and herb garden. Late morning, I shower and prepare a wholefood lunch. After lunch, I work in the studio or collect plants for weaving, combined with other tasks. In the evening, I work by the fireside on fibre art projects until late, listening to music. I watch no TV. I live alone so can leave my work set up ready for the next day.

*What traditional 'heritage' methods do you use in your craft?*
I grow and harvest Australian indigenous plants for use in fibre art. I use ancient and simple stitching techniques.

*How have you adapted heritage or historic methods for the modern day?*
I use ancient but simple stitching techniques to create original modern pieces rather than traditional designs. I don't follow patterns or templates. I work from imagination and innovate to solve design challenges.

*What advice would you give someone starting out in your field?*
Look at what is happening in broader fibre art and craft practice, don't be isolated, and keep going. It takes a lot of time, but it is time well spent. I enjoy the culture of sharing in craft practice. I often imagine that I am channelling something very ancient, even though the finished work may be new and modern. It helps me to feel part of a larger culture of creative endeavour; I am not isolated or alone in my work.

## About me:
I am a visual artist and nature conservationist and I live and work at Venus Bay, Victoria on the South East coast of Australia. Here I own and manage an Advanced Ecotourism accommodation business called Venus Bay Eco Retreat. My home, workshop and studio are located on this property.

The land is 5.6 hectares of pristine coastal bushland managed with a Trust for Nature conservation covenant, this is a voluntary covenant that protects biodiversity in perpetuity on privately owned land. My fibre art work is inspired by the landscape I live in and by my desire to create sustainable and innovative art work that celebrates the unique beauty of the Australian landscape.

Website: *http://www.venusbay-ecoretreat.com.au/*
Instagram: *mae_venusbayecoretreat*
Facebook: *www.facebook.com/vbecoretreat*
Email: *mae@skymesh.com.au*

## Joanna Blythe – Limegreenjelly

*What first attracted you to your craft?*
I had a long history of making; making art, painting silk, sewing clothing. I studied design at college but got into yarn and knitting in my twenties.

*Can you describe your journey into your craft? How did you get started? For example, do you have particular training or qualifications, or are you self-taught?*
I left school and was pushed into graphic design by a well-meaning art teacher. On leaving college I did many varied jobs and some part-time courses. I completed a City and Guilds in Fashion and had hoped to do a textiles degree. Life and responsibilities got in the way. I also went back to college in my 30s to do a Foundation Course, again with the plan to do a textiles degree and life again, or the starting of a family, got in the way this time!

My son was one and I was asked to set up a local knitting group in Hastings where I was living, shortly after that someone was offering fleeces on a local Freecycle group. I collected some fleeces and found a local lady through the Guild of Spinners, Weavers and Dyers who gave me a spinning lesson and that really was the start... I wasn't spinning white fleece for long, I moved into dyeing my own wool and spinning one-of-a-kind yarns. Weaving followed a bit later after I had joined my local Guild of Spinners, Weavers and Dyers and after being inspired by the Get Weaving ladies at my first Woolfest as a vendor!

*Do you have any inspirations or influences? This could include particular artisans, periods in history etc.*
Colour is my main influence, I love playing with colour and seeing what happens. I work in an instinctive free way when it comes to colours and fibres in weaving, dyeing and spinning.

*What do you enjoy most about working with the materials that you choose to work with?*
It comes down to colour, and mixing, what I do can be full of surprises and happy accidents as colours mix together in a yarn or woven fabric.

*Please describe the tools of your craft, and how you use them.*
I use a Majacraft Little Gem spinning wheel, most of the fibres I spin are next to skin soft like merino wools and luxury blends that I have dyed myself, with acid dyes and steam fixed in my kitchen. I have two Saori floor looms. I use them both for weaving a variety of fabrics, scarves and shawls.

*Describe your business. What items do you make? Do you sell items – if so, what? Do you teach courses? Describe the thing you have made that has made you most proud.*
I don't really consider myself a business. I do sell my work but items take quite a bit of time to make and I do not work and sell fast enough to earn a living from what I do. I make scarves, shawls, lavender bags, I have made

bags, handwoven purses, notebook covers. I sell hand-painted yarns, fibre for other spinners and felt makers and handspun yarn too.

The thing that makes me most proud is just being an advocate for making and creating and experimenting and sharing my knowledge with others to help them forward. I don't do much teaching as time is limited but I feel that any kind of creative activity is good for mind and body and want to make sure we don't lose sight of that in the future.

*Please describe a typical day.*
School run, housework, weaving, dyeing, knitting, photography, occasionally listing items and admin.

*What traditional heritage methods do you use in your craft?*
I'm not 100 per cent sure what you mean by heritage methods…I can use a drop spindle, or even a weighted stick for spinning. The looms I use are modern but still traditional using the age–old design.

*What advice would you give someone starting out in your field?*
This is a difficult question to answer. You need to be sure exactly what you want to gain from your craft and if you want to make a living from it you need to be aware of things like creative burn out. I feel lucky to be in a place where I can choose to do what I want to do. There is no pressure on me to have to sell, sell, sell or produce items quickly. There is a usually a demand for classes. You need to think carefully; some people find that they end up spending all their time teaching, with no time for making and experimenting. You don't always get paid for every hour you spent making something. Some of my handspun yarns can take ten hours to spin 100g. You just need to be clear with what you are doing and why.

I think if you really want to make a successful profitable business you have to be completely single minded. Some of the best advice I was given was to stick to one thing and at the time I did really stick with the dyeing and the business grew and I was shipping fibres all over the world. On the flip side of this I found some of the jobs tedious and was on a constant hamster wheel of dyeing, sorting, photographing, listing, packing and posting. Some people would rather be on that hamster wheel than working in an office, I guess now I'm just lucky to be able to choose what I do.

For me making isn't about selling. I make because I love the process, its good for my mind, it calms me, it enriches my being. You could strip away all the yarn and equipment from my life and I would still be making in some form, with pen and paper, scissors, collage; it's not just part of me, it's who I am. I am an artisan, I don't understand people who have no hobbies or interests.

## About me:

I am 48, I live in Suffolk. I have a husband and two sons. I have a crafty mum who can sew a silk purse from a sow's ear and I'm just a happy dabbler. I weave, knit, sew, dye and draw. Since most of my creative obsessions involve sitting around eating cake and talking about wool I have also taken up running, just to ensure that I will be able to indulge my interests for many years to come.

Facebook: *limegreenjelly*

Instagram: *limegreenwelly*

Etsy shop: *by limegreenjelly*

## Gilleoin Finlay-Coull – Woolrush

*What first attracted you to your craft?*

I suppose you could say I was attracted to it even before I was born, as my father was an internationally known craftsman in the fields of ceramics and stained glass. He had originally wanted to study textiles but changed

Gilleoin Finlay-Coull's logo for her business, *Woolrush*.

The beautiful wheel made by Gilleoin's talented father. It was a copy of a very old spinning wheel made for the 1951 British Empire exhibition.

direction. My mother was also an excellent craftsman, but as was common with that generation, she stayed at home to care for the family.

*Describe your journey into your craft. How did you get started? Do you have training or qualifications or are you self-taught?*

My father was commissioned to make a free copy of a very old spinning wheel for the 1951 British Empire exhibition, the original being too fragile for display. He was to keep the wheel after the exhibition finished. It came to live in our house, at the top of the stairway and from a very early age, probably about three or four years old, it fascinated me and I always wanted to play with it. At that age, I couldn't reach the treadle, as my legs were too short. I made up my mind that as soon as I was big enough, I would learn to use it properly. In the meantime, aged four, I learned to knit and soon had the best-dressed dolls in the street, despite wool and fabric still being difficult to obtain, as this was less than a decade after the end of the Second World War. Knitting patterns (or sewing ones, for that matter) for dolls were also almost impossible to come by, so with Mum's help, I learned to make up simple patterns for myself, using scraps of fabric and yarn saved by neighbours, as well as by Mum. Dad would draw out shapes for me as 'patterns' and as I grew older, would make suggestions as to where I could improve my 'designs'.

When I left school, I went on to university and took an academic degree, but still continued to knit, although spinning fell by the wayside a little, there being only so many hours in the day! After graduating and getting married, there was a marked lack of employment opportunities for someone with my slightly peculiar skill set, so I began to take knitting commissions. Icelandic sweaters were very much in demand and I soon found myself working on commission for a handloom weaver friend in the Highlands, as well as work for a well-known company in the Scottish Borders.

My formal qualifications had no bearing on my textile career, but you could say that I had had training from a very early age. I taught myself to spin on Dad's wheel at the age of 12 and he taught me to weave on a small rigid heddle loom. The weaving was put aside eventually, as spinning, designing and knitting absorbed most of my available time. Later dyeing, crochet, Dorset button-making and needle-felting skills would be added, but only as 'sidelines', with the exception of the dyeing, which is complementary to the spinning.

*What are your inspirations or influences – e.g. particular artisans or periods of history?*

I can't say that there is any one person, apart from my parents, who influenced me. I did study quite extensively the industrialisation of the textile industry from the cottage industry based in everyday living in past ages as part of my degree. Most of my inspiration comes from the natural world around me, which inspires the colours and blends of colours I use in my yarns and also shapes and patterns of shapes in creating knitted garments and other items.

*What do you enjoy most about the materials you use?*

The tactile nature of the materials I use and the way different fibres take up dye and the endless possibilities of colour and texture in the end results of yarn and knitting.

*Describe the tools of your craft and how you use them*

The main tools of spinning are a drum carder (or hand cards for sampling blends of colour); the spinning wheel; the Lazy Kate; the Niddy Noddy; the Swift; knitting needles.

The drum carder (or hand cards) is covered in a carding cloth which is a rubberised base 'cloth' covered in metal spines set in rows

Gilleoin's hand carder, for carding fibre into batts, ready to spin.

at specific intervals, these vary from a coarse cloth to a fine cloth and different drums are used for different purposes. I have a wool carder that has interchangeable drums which gives me great flexibility when carding different fibres. It is hand operated, although electric ones are available.

My spinning wheel – I mostly use a modern double treadle Scotch tension upright wheel, which is similar in shape to the Orkney wheel.

The Lazy Kate is a free-standing tool with usually three spindles, onto which the full bobbins from the wheel are placed so that the yarn from each can be plied onto the bobbin on the wheel. I usually just use two bobbins to create two-ply yarn in various weights, the end thickness being determined by the thickness of the 'singles' – i.e. the single thread spun on each bobbin.

Gilleoin's Lazy Kate and Niddy Noddy. The Lazy Kate is a free-standing tool onto which full bobbins of yarn are placed, and can be plied onto the bobbin on the wheel to create two-ply or three-ply yarn. The Niddy Noddy is used to wind the plied yarn onto to make a hank or skein.

The Niddy Noddy is a vertical shaft with 'arms' top and bottom, the top ones being at 90 degrees from the bottom one and is used to wind the plied yarn onto to make a hank or skein.

The Swift is the tool for winding off the hank into balls. It can either be vertical, with rollers one above the other with the ability to be adjusted as appropriate to the length of the hank, or the umbrella type, which is horizontal and also adjustable.

Knitting needles for the garments. I use metal or wood straight, single pointed or double pointed, or plastic circular needles, depending on what I'm making.

*Describe your business. What items do you make? Do you sell work and if so what? Do you teach? Please describe an item you have made that has made you most proud.*

I am an independent craftsman working entirely alone. I spin my own range of natural fibre yarns, mostly wool and sourced from the UK. The yarns are branded as Woolrush Handspun Yarns. I also dye many of my yarns using both natural and acid dyes. I design my own knitwear, making the samples and writing the patterns, for both adults and baby/toddler sizes. The adult range is The Calanas Collection – the word 'Calanas' in Gaelic means the processing of fleece from the sheep to the finished item. The baby range is The Woolly Lamb Collection. I also make traditional Dorset buttons, including a design exclusive to me. I sell my yarns, patterns, buttons and finished garments.

I teach infrequently now and usually only on a one-to-one basis, as I no longer have premises suitable for teaching larger groups, nor the equipment.

I have made so much in the course of a long career, that it is almost impossible to pick out any one thing that I could say made me most proud. I have spun, designed and knitted several christening shawls and many years ago I designed and knitted, using traditional methods,

Dorset Rose Buttons
by Gilleoin.

two Shetland 'Knit Frocks' – the traditional Shetland equivalent of the Fisherman's Gansey, using Fair Isle patterns.

*Please describe a typical day.*

I don't really have a 'typical' day. I usually spend between three and six hours spinning or otherwise preparing fibre. Knitting, making buttons and pattern writing tends to get fitted in on a less regular basis, although I try to knit a little each day to relax!

I don't work a set 'nine to five' day, as I have other aspects in my life that require my attention, so the hours I spend working on fibre related things (and they are many more than just the amount mentioned above) are distributed throughout the day and evening.

*What traditions or heritage methods do you use?*

Most of what I do is traditional as are most of the tools I use. Some things, like the Scotch tension and double treadle on my wheel and the drum carder are more 'modern' innovations, but still in the tradition of the past. I hand knit the garments I make and the Dorset buttons are lodged

Dorset Pinwheel Buttons
by Gilleoin.

in a long heritage, going back to the eighteenth century and before, when Dorset was the centre for button making in England

*How have you adapted heritage methods to the modern day?*
Apart from the adaptations of the spinning wheel and the drum carder mentioned above and the use of gas/electricity to heat the dye baths, most of the work I do and the tools and methods I use would be recognisable to craftsmen of old and I see no reason to update that. There are domestic electric spinners available and knitting machines, both manual and electronic, but I have no inclination to adopt them. I pride myself on being a true hand craftsman in the old tradition.

*What advice would you give to someone starting out in your field?*
If you enjoy working with fibre and yarn as a hobby, be very sure that your love of the craft is strong enough to carry the pressures of doing it as a business. It is not a 'nine to five' job and will not make you rich, nor give you endless free time but it will give you flexibility and a great deal of satisfaction.

Gilleoin's current spinning wheel.

**About me:**

I was born less than a decade after the end of the second world war. My father was an internationally known designer craftsman in the fields of ceramics and stained glass, although he began his career in textiles. He, along with other friends, was instrumental in reviving studio pottery in Scotland after the war. My mother was also an excellent craftsman in textiles but did not pursue her career. I therefore grew up in a world which revolved round art and craft of varying types. Knitting and sewing were everyday necessities at that time, as there was little choice available commercially in the way of clothing and household textiles, so I learned these skills at the age of four. As soon as I was tall enough for my feet to reach the treadle, I taught myself to spin, using fleece that we collected from fences and hedgerows. In later years, I was able to source fleece from local farmers. I continued to knit, design and spin while studying for an academic degree in history and Scottish studies. Having completed my degree, I began my career as a 'cottage' industry, adding the skills of dyeing, crochet, freeform and other textile related skills. Many years on, I continue to create products in fibre and yarn. I draw my inspiration from the shapes, colours and patterns in the natural everyday world around me and strive to continue the historic traditions that have fascinated me all my life and to create my products using traditional methods.

Website: *www.woolrush.weebly.com*
Facebook: *www.facebook.com/woolrush*
Etsy shop: *www.etsy.com/shop/woolrush*
Folksy: *www.folksy.com/shop/woolrush*
Email: *spinninggill@aol.co.uk*

**Tracy Calderbank**

*What first attracted you to your craft?*

I love the colours and textures it creates in textiles, in photography it's the light and dark, with ceramic and sculpture it's the shapes made.

*Can you describe your journey into your craft? How did you get started? For example, do you have particular training or qualifications, or are you self-taught?*

If I could have been born with a pencil in my hand then I would have! I've been drawing and colouring since early childhood. I was happiest when I was sitting in a corner with a pencil and paper. I received the standard teaching of art in school (I helped the others) such as the GCSE and 'A' levels and from there I continued down the road into a diploma in design, having a taste of wood work and ceramics, but mostly drawing and painting.

From there I had a break from education, but my interest shifted towards the craft side of the arts such as jewellery making and sewing. I fell into the world of cross stitch – the counted type not the printed pattern type. This got me back painting with the idea of designing my own cross stitch images.

I think it was this that opened the road again to education. I enrolled on a BA degree in fine art, gaining a 2:1. In this way my crafting moved on to the digital side of things, photography becoming my medium of choice. While studying for my degree I worked in a studio with other artists and crafters, and I was introduced to weaving, along with spinning. I loved it so much that I was given a 22 inch rigid heddle loom, and I then invested in a 32 inch loom and an inkle loom. I was shown how to warp up then left to experiment, so much so that I have now bought a drop spindle from Yarndale. I'm working on buying a spinning wheel eventually.

*Do you have any inspirations or influences? This could include particular artisans, periods in history etc.*

On the art side I'm drawn to art nouveau and art deco for the flow of nouveau curves and the architectural side of art deco. With photography it's Ansel Adams and Charles Rennie Mackintosh, with the jewellery and architecture. This influences my work. With my interests in jewellery, ceramic, photography, and textiles, I think overall it's the colours that are created and blended.

*Please describe the tools of your craft, and how you use them.*
The tools of my craft vary from the digital camera and computer, to the rigid heddle loom, pencil and paper.

How I use these also varies. I jump into my gallery of images taken, as they can inspire an idea…or the colours of wool for the loom. The various types of beads I use which can be used to make jewellery or woven either on the loom (big one) or the small beading loom. With the ceramics I sketch ideas out first from images seen from the photos taken.

*Describe your business. What items do you make? Do you sell items – if so, what? Do you teach courses? Describe the thing you have made that has made you most proud.*
I don't have a building at the moment, as yet, but it's on the list of things to do. I love to make a variety of things from jewellery, ceramic pots, pendants and beads to woven scarfs, covers and bags. I am planning to run courses; they are on my list of things to sort out for the future...

What made me proud was the poncho that I wove on my loom and the bag that I lined with felt.

*Please describe a typical day.*
A typical day of creating: a large mug of Ceylon tea, music in the background. If it's a day of starting a project, then it's to the computer to be inspired by the many photos taken from whatever caught my eye – the colours, light, angle or texture.

If the project is already in progress then it's slipping back into the zone and continue weaving on the rigid heddle loom, inkle loom and drop spindle. (Hoping for a spinning wheel eventually.) Teaching myself how to use a lucet to make braids.

*What advice would you give someone starting out in your field?*
My advice is to try different things; experiment; don't get stuck in one field unless you want to – but at least try things – but most of all have fun. If it's not fun then don't do it.

## About me:

Throughout my life and in all of my work experiences I am a lifelong advocate of learning, personal development and well-being. Working from home means I can manage my time to do things I enjoy too and develop my business as a craft person. I have young grandchildren who love to get involved in my craft work and will ask to spin and weave. I have a small VW campervan and nothing gives me more pleasure than heading off in Daisy van with my spinning wheel and parking up somewhere quiet and scenic and spending time enjoying my craft.

Coming from the Welsh hills I believe I have fleece in my genetic makeup and used to sit around the open fire as a child whilst my family chatted and knitted. I trained as a complementary therapist at Napier University, achieving a BSc at the age of 49 whilst working full time, so I am quite driven and enjoy challenges and new adventures. My love of sharing skills has led me down the path of running workshops and classes my whole working life, from Learning and Developmental manager through to self-employed training consultant in subjects relevant to people working in Health and Social Care. This has transferred to sharing craft skills with others and promoting well-being through crafts.

## Katie Mairis – Yarn for the Soul

*What first attracted you to your craft?*
I learnt to dye yarn because I adore colour and texture. I am able to create the texture through crochet and knitting, but to be able to add my own colour and depth means such a lot.

*Can you describe your journey into your craft? How did you get started? For example, do you have particular training or qualifications, or are you self-taught?*

I am completely self-taught. I also taught myself to crochet, knit and dye.

*Do you have any inspirations or influences? This could include particular artisans, periods in history etc.*

I love Art Noveau and Art Deco. I love the linear and curvature, the softness and boldness of colours... Lalique and Mackintosh. Then, from one extreme to another but in modern terms, I admire O'Keefe and Mondrian.... perhaps the nouveau and the deco of a different era with linear structure and nature influencing both of them.

*What do you enjoy most about working with the materials that you choose to work with?*

I love the fact that I work with my hands. When I wind my yarn into a ball I use a wooden swift.... not a modern machine with batteries. When I dye my yarn, I use my hands. My business is a real cottage industry. It's just me in my kitchen. I am proud of that. I am proud that I can run my business in a modern era using a traditional cottage industry.

*What tradition 'heritage' methods do you use in your craft?*

I use a wooden Amish swift to wind skeins of yarn into balls. I use a manual winder to cake the yarn, or I use my hands. I use crochet hooks and knitting needles. I also use skeins of merino yarn or yak and silk or cashmere. I soak them in a solution of citric acid before dyeing them individually, by hand and then steaming the skeins individually. When cool I rinse them and hang them to dry on my washing line. When dry

I then twist each skein by hand. I hand dye yarn and I sell yarn dyed by myself and a few other indie dyers.

I also sell knitting needles and crochet hooks, notions and patterns as well as yarn care products. I don't teach courses but I will be running workshops very soon where groups can have a go at dyeing yarn themselves. I started this business after a stay in hospital where I noticed that flowers were not allowed on wards anymore and people were flocking to see my project. When I was well again I set up my business which started out sending project parcels to people who were incapacitated. It has grown and grown. I have done this on my own. That is what has made me feel most proud.

*How have you adapted heritage or historic methods for the modern day?*
I try to do most things in the most traditional methods. For me the most traditional part is the lack of machinery and the fact I do it all myself and by hand. Every skein is dyed by hand. It is steamed and rinsed by me, by hand. Then dried and wound. Even though I do everything by hand I have modernised the process by using cling film and a microwave to speed up the steaming process.

*What advice would you give someone starting out in your field?*
My advice would be this...don't be shy. Be bold. You can do it. Ask for opinions and take advice on board.

### About me:
I'm 38 and a mum to Rosie (11) and Ruby (7).
Website: *www.yarnforthesoul.co.uk*
Instagram: *yarnforthesoul*
Facebook: *yarnforthesoul*

Carol Gascoigne's beautiful Alpaca fleece ready to be spun on her wheel.

**Carole Gascoigne – Craftywoman**

*What first attracted you to your craft?*

Born in a small Welsh village surrounded by fields of sheep and having a mother who made all my clothes, both sewing and knitting and later on in life spinning, I believe it is in my genetic makeup. I remember having my first weaving loom as a child and making numerous blankets for my dolls. I also learned to knit at a young age. When I first left home and set off in the world on my own the first thing I bought was a sewing machine.

I have always been involved in self-empowerment and well-being and found that craft work allowed me to forget day-to-day concerns and to become fully absorbed in the art of spinning, weaving or felting, which have therapeutic benefits.

*Can you describe your journey into your craft? How did you get started? For example, do you have particular training or qualifications, or are you self-taught?*

I have always been busy with crafts, either through what I learned as a child at home, self-taught or through attending workshops.

I studied foundation art for a year, then went on to complete two years of a City and Guilds creative embroidery course at Telford college. Whilst doing my creative embroidery course I had a visit to the Dovecot tapestry workshop in Edinburgh and this completely inspired me. The craftsmanship, use of pattern and colour was just beautiful – it was also during this time that I had my first foray into felting.

About three years ago I eventually bought my first rigid heddle loom, and then my first spinning wheel and spindle and started spinning my own fibres. I learned how to spin and weave with the Haddington Spinners and Weavers in East Lothian, then later joined the Edinburgh Weavers, Spinners and Dyers Guild. Since then I have developed my skills further and attended workshops amongst others on stick spinning, inkle loom weaving and botanical printing.

I am an active member of an online forum, The Felt and Fibre Studio and have featured in their blog spot a few times: http://feltandfiberstudio. proboards.com/

*Do you have any inspirations or influences? This could include particular artisans, periods in history etc.*
I don't have anyone in particular, it is more a mix of talented people who have inspired me with their own enthusiasm, processes and journeys, from people who dye using natural plant dyes and mushroom dyes to people who weave, spin and then create their own garments.

*What do you enjoy most about working with the materials that you choose to work with?*
I enjoy how you can create the yarn you want depending on your project, how to develop your work and I also enjoy the technical side of understanding design and pattern as well as the alchemy of dyeing. For wet felting, although you have a modicum of control, it is also the organic process of how things change and develop as you felt.

*Please describe the tools of your craft, and how you use them.*
The start of my journey began with felting, initially wet felting 2D before moving on to 3D objects. In the beginning, I mainly made wet felted pieces that I embellished, so I made lots of pods, some with beading, some with embroidery and some with embellishments. Then I taught myself to needle felt and developed this skill by using wire armatures to create sloths, a donkey and many other creatures. The tools you need for felting are pretty straightforward. I use bubble wrap, a bamboo table mat, water and soap. To make a 3D object you include a resist, which is a thin piece of a fabric that doesn't felt. When I learned to embellish I started using felting needles of different sizes to create

the effects I wanted. I then developed my needle felting skills to make 3D animals.

I use a rigid Heddle Knitter's loom, which on the surface seems quite straightforward but you can do all sorts of things with it. I bought attachments for double weaving, which means you can double the width of your weaving or you can weave a tube. I use an Ashford Traveller's spinning wheel, which I bought to learn the basics of spinning, but it is versatile so I have continued with it but I am tempted by other wheels, especially ones that can be folded. In my campervan I enjoy spinning in a range of lovely settings such as looking over the sea or sitting in the mountains and if it rains I can still sit in my van and spin. The last time I was travelling with my van and spinning I was approached by a woman who had huskies and she asked me to spin a bag of husky fur, which I did by mixing it with another fibre – the end result was one happy husky owner and another convert to spinning.

I use a carder to mix fibres and create colour combinations that appeal to me. (A carder is a round drum that you feed fibres into and you can mix and add fibres ready for with spinning or making into felt).

I have other bits of kit which allow me to make skeins from my spun yarn, first using a niddy-noddy to create the skeins, then putting them onto a swift before attaching them to a ball winder and ending up with balls of yarn.

*Describe your business. What items do you make? Do you sell items – if so, what? Do you teach courses? Describe the thing you have made that has made you most proud.*

As I don't work full time at my craft I only make one-off pieces that a local art gallery takes and sells for me. My main interest is in teaching others. I have run courses in wet felting, scarf making, Nuno felting and needle felting 3D pieces.

The item I am most proud of is my first alpaca shawl. I bought a kilo of white alpaca fleece, spun it in the dirt (which means I didn't wash it first) and, when the skeins were ready, I washed it and dyed them. Once dyed, I wove the skeins and then bravely cut them and made them into an asymmetrical wrap lined with shocking pink fabric.

*Please describe a typical day.*
A typical day possibly includes either washing fleece, carding fleece, spinning fleece – I do like using Shetland – and leaving it flat to dry. While spinning fibres such as Shetland I also spin alpaca, merino and silk, often I will be exploring ideas for developing felting pieces, new woven pieces, or trying my hand at a new skill such as tapestry weaving or embroidery. I seem to have quite a few projects on the go at any time. I am currently experimenting with transferring images onto fabric and then layering the fabric on to a cotton wadding and hand stitching into the image to create a new effect.

Although not typical, but certainly interesting, was a day with the Haddington Spinners and Weavers on International Women's Day, outside the Scottish Parliament building, spinning. This event was to raise awareness of women and craft whilst also having a political message about women and equality. This was following on from inappropriate comments made by Donald Trump, so as a group we knitted hats made from our own spun and dyed yarn in protest (the movement is called 'craftivism') to his negative comments about women. We also had a slot on Women's Hour talking about this event.

*What tradition 'heritage' methods do you use in your craft?*
I use spinning crafts, both with a spinning wheel and a spindle, felting, weaving, and dyeing using natural dyes methods. I had the absolute pleasure of learning how to waulk the tweed, a traditional method of

finishing off freshly woven tweed cloth. Traditionally it involved a group of women rhythmically beating newly woven tweed whilst singing waulking songs. I did this with a group from Inverclyde, on the west coast of Scotland. Their name, *Sgioba Luaidh Inbhirchluaidh*, means Inverclyde Waulking Group.

*How have you adapted heritage or historic methods for the modern day?*
I use modern-day tools which, although certainly not heritage, are based on the original tools, such as my spinning wheel and my loom. Originally an open fire would have been used to heat the water for making the dye, whereas I use a steamer or microwave. I pick plants from my garden or when out on walks, and I collect fallen lichen for dyeing. Talking of spinning, I have learned how to stick spin, so that involves picking up a piece of natural wood and using it as a spinner and tying sticks together to make a spindle too. So no matter where I am out

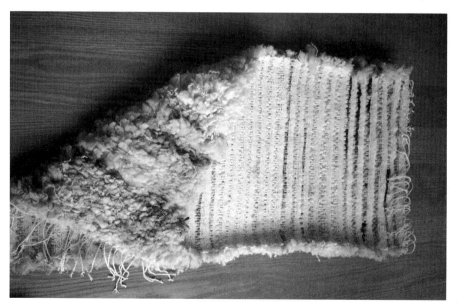

Gorgeous, textured fibre rug woven by Carol Gascoigne.

in nature I can collect fleece from the fences and spin yarn, I can boil plants on a camping stove and dye the yarn and if I have needles with me I could knit it up too.

*What advice would you give someone starting out in your field?*
I would highly recommend joining a Guild or a group who meet and share skills; you learn so much from other people and the guild's aim is to share skills and even loan out equipment to get you started. It is reasonably-priced and offers many opportunities to expand on your learning, also a great source of knowledge of equipment, fleeces and processes. There are many classes in a wide range of subjects and again a good place to start. Personally, I found being around like-minded people inspired me and expanded my knowledge and experiences.
Facebook: *craftywomanScotland*
Blog: *https://craftybeetle.wordpress.com/*

## Zoe Robson – FLEECE4EWE

*What first attracted you to your craft?*
I was attracted to wool mainly after moving to Scotland sixteen years ago this June. We had rare breed sheep and I wanted to use their wool.

*Can you describe your journey into your craft? How did you get started? For example, do you have particular training or qualifications, or are you self-taught?*
I'm interested in lots of crafts but especially wool. I knitted a lot as a young adult, but then had a bit of a lull. After moving to Scotland, I started selling our Blackwelsh fleece straight off the sheep, but really I just wanted to see it being used. I didn't have enough fleece to send to the Wool Board. I then started sorting it and selling it at first on eBay. The more you work sorting and handling fleece, the more you become

naturally more aware of what makes good and bad fleece, and which wool is good for what purpose. So I have no particular qualifications in this field or training – but lots of experience!

*Do you have any inspirations or influences? This could include particular artisans, periods in history etc.*

I have no particular inspirations, apart from trying to promote rare breed sheep and fleece and trying to encourage folk to buy wool from the UK.

*What do you enjoy most about working with the materials that you choose to work with?*

I love working with all wool, especially the natural lovely coloured fleeces as they are all so unique. I also love blending and carding colours and am good at matching animal colours for needle felters.

*Please describe the tools of your craft, and how you use them.*

My main tool is myself and having a good eye for nice quality raw fleece – and then the ability to hand sort and process it. My main machine I wouldn't be without is my electric wool carder.

*Describe your business. What items do you make? Do you sell items – if so, what? Do you teach courses? Describe the thing you have made that has made you most proud.*

My business is FLEECE4EWE. I mainly make carded wools and blends now for my customers for them to craft which leaves little time for me to craft. I do make needle felted 3D and 2D things and felted cards. I spin my own wool have knitted cushions and hats etc, and have crocheted my own patterned shawls. I also make peg loom rugs. I have recently started teaching beginners needle felting at our local ethical gift shop which is proving popular. I plan a peg loom workshop later in the year. I am very proud to have washed and spun my own wool and then crocheted it into a shawl.

*Please describe a typical day.*
A typical day sees me get up and see to the sheep which could be anything from feeding, lambing or checking them, depending on time of year. I walk the collies and then have breakfast. Then I go out to craft and prepare any orders.

Around 10.30am I have a coffee break – but that's sometimes on the hoof! After that, I continue with my orders. I card wool especially for people according to their needs. If there are no orders to process, or when I am done, I love to card wool and make coloured blends of different types of fibre in different colour and texture blends, which I then try to sell later in the day.

Then I pack wool, sort wool or cut up tweed into pieces for needle felting clients, or I wash more wool. At noon I have my lunch but only give myself around twenty minutes. Then I am back to wool sorting. Around 4pm most days I start to take photos of the wools I have carded to put online at tea time. My hubby comes home and we have a quick coffee; then it's time for normal sheep duties, checking them again etc. After I cook tea and wash up, it's time to list things to sell online, pack up any more orders ready to post the day after. I pride myself in sending orders quickly. I feed the sheep again, then walk the dogs again – and then it's house work – sometimes!

I make up special packs to sell, and sit and network some more online, on my phone. It seems like a lot, but it is where I get most of my business. Then I order stock such as packaging while glancing at the tv. Occasionally I even have time to craft myself! Last thing I do is have a snack and a bath; walk the dogs again, and lock the chickens up before finally going to bed.

*How have you adapted heritage or historic methods for the modern day?*
I still traditionally hand wash wool. Things have not changed much – it's still a sink and hard work. In the olden times they would have used hand carders to card wool, but now I use an electric carder which is much better, especially time wise.

*What advice would you give someone starting out in your field?*
If you are starting out with raw fleece, buy quality fleece that's been well sorted and well looked after and be prepared to pay for quality. In the end it saves you time and actually is cheaper in the long run.

## About me:

My first encounter with sheep was when I met my husband who kept sheep! I ordered hay off him for my ponies and he delivered it. Things blossomed and he took me to a livestock sheep sale, and I took him to a horse sale – and the rest is history!

I then bought my first sheep. They were small white Welsh mountains, in lamb. The bug started that time we were in Yorkshire renting land and had many a breed. Hubby worked on an arable and livestock farm and was good with sheep. We got the chance to move up to Scotland sixteen years ago, and we bought a wee croft with three acres. We still rented land and have had lots of breeds of sheep. I have had heaps of different jobs but always come back to my crafting. I took the plunge and gave up my good job at a local school to concentrate on my FLEECE4EWE business, as I was always busy and working long hours. It's great being at home and doing what I love. I'm lucky that my husband, who now works as a postie for Royal Mail, has a full time job and supports me. He gave up farming due to his boss retiring and he also suffered with a neck injury.

My business started small, but I'm busy enough now. I don't think it can grow much more as I want it to remain the case that I give a personal service to my customers. It's great that wool is having a revival and you can do such a lot with it! It is great to use UK fleece from our lovely sheep too. We now keep rare breeds and are members of RBS. We are also members of the northern support group and attend local shows and help promote breeds and I do demos with wool. We also enjoy showing the sheep and have had great success. I've learned a lot but am still learning. I've also learned it is much cheaper to buy fleece then it is to keep sheep for their fleece! Ho hum! I hope I'm encouraging people along the way to enjoy the love of wool and join the addictive wool buying, carding and spinning.

You can only find me on Facebook on my woolly page Fleece 4 ewe. I've got two website domains but no website as I don't have time to spend stocking one at present. I've lots to see and buy on my woolly page or people message me for what they need and I try to help them with a personal touch. I don't have a bricks and mortar shop, but I post to UK and abroad. I have stalls at three wool festivals this year. I also regularly put sales of wool on the Facebook group for all things woolly, Needlefelt UK. Email: *fleece4ewe@gmail.com*

## Tamsin Juby – B F Fiber Arts Creations, Ontario

My name is Tammy Juby. I'm a fiber artist in general. I crochet, process fleeces from raw, dye yarns (both handspun and mill spun), spin, felt and I'm learning knitting.

I began crocheting as a way to deal with nerves. I had tried knitting and found it was too complex for me but I was drawn to yarn in a visceral way. I loved the colors and the feel and I needed to do something so I could use it. I picked up a book on how to crochet, some plastic crochet hooks, a few balls of Red Heart Yarn and started playing. Crochet was my jam. Pretty soon I had a SABLE – stash accumulation beyond life expectancy – and I couldn't stop making things!

Then I discovered hand dyed yarns from small companies. I was so in love. In my usual way, I gave hand dyeing mill spun yarn a try. What fun! There had to be more to learn.

I was obsessed with the differences between fibres and started studying the making of yarn. I got the bright idea to try spinning. I found a decorative wheel (one that wasn't actually designed to spin), purchased the head for a Lendrum wheel, cobbled them together with bungee cords and started spinning. I called that first wheel 'Frank', for Frankenstein of course. I had no fear trying this. People have been spinning fibers for hundreds of years. They've made equipment to do what they want. If I had any skills with wood, I probably would have made my own wheel. You can't be afraid to try things, to make do with what you have on hand. A drop spindle is the simplest tool there is and while I have still to master the skill, it's a portable spinning device you can make from a stick. How amazing is that?

I'm attempting to learn the techniques of Andean spinning. They spin all day long while walking and talking and the fact that they've done it this way for hundreds of years is simply inspiring. I've just purchased a raw Romney fleece that I intend to prepare and spin on a drop spindle using these techniques. To be able to use the simplest tools to make such functional yarn just challenges me to push myself.

'Frank' and I had a wonderful affair for a year before I realized this obsession wasn't going away. So, I bought a Lendrum spinning wheel, named him 'Lars' and we've been married ever since. With the help of YouTube and videos from Interweave I tackled more and more complex yarns. The first thing I learned was everyone had opinions on the 'proper' way to do things, quite often contradictory opinions. The best part about being self taught was I didn't have an instructor preventing me from trying everything and deciding what worked best for me. But it still wasn't enough! There was more to learn.

I found a local sheep farmer who raises her flock more as pets than as farm animals and I purchased my first raw fleeces. Oh my, what a rabbit hole! The smell of the fleece, the way it all hangs together straight off the sheep, a new obsession. If you've never touched a fleece still warm from the animal you are missing an experience. The wool will never feel so soft, the lanolin will never be so fluid. It's an amazing sensation. But to use the fleece, it had to be cleaned. Time to do some more learning on how to scour fleece, then card and comb to prepare it for spinning.

Tools haven't changed much over the years. They may be fancier or made of better woods and steel but the concepts remain the same. Hand cards are covered in small pins that open the fleece while removing vegetable matter and dirt, best for making airy yarn. Combs have long, wickedly sharp tines that straighten all the fibers, lining them all up in the same direction and making for a denser yarn when spinning. Experimenting with both ways of preparing fiber is the best way to learn which breeds of sheep and length of fibers is best for both methods. A quick Google search can lead you to hundreds of methods for making your own combs to get you started. People have even used cactuses to comb fleece so be creative and use what's on hand. That's the same way heritage artists discovered how to do things; with experimentation. Don't be afraid to try things. The sheep are always growing more wool. It's a fully renewable resource.

As I acquired more and more fleece, I purchased a drum carder for processing the pounds I had but I was just as likely to use my trusty hand cards. Well, at this point, I had more fiber and fiber related products than I could ever use so I dipped my toe into craft fairs and began selling supplies to local craft people and finished items to the ones who just wanted to enjoy the finished product. With trial and error, I established a loyal customer base locally and started working on expanding that outwards into the larger world with my Facebook page.

People are becoming more and more aware of the source of what they purchase and being able to show them a picture of the sheep their gloves came from connects them to the product in a way Walmart can't. The importance of traditional methods of producing goods is forefront in people's minds these days and while life can be too busy for them to do it themselves, they are willing to pay to have it done for them. This is an ever-expanding market for traditional artists. Shows became educational opportunities and I discovered I really enjoy doing demonstrations of spinning and sharing my love of all things fiber. This lead to my YouTube channel so I could share with even more people.

I had a lot of customers for dyed, combed fibers who were felters so I became curious and tried doing that as well. Since I handle all steps of the process myself, I've been able to make felted shawls in ways that most felters cannot, simply because they generally work with prepared fleeces. My curly lock shawls have been very popular. I simply experimented with methods until I found a way that works for me. How it is done I can't share as it's a secret recipe like Big Mac Sauce.

Unfortunately, life throws us curve balls and my spouse became chronically ill and I have less time to devote to my fiber crafts these days. But they've become even more important for keeping me calm and happy as we navigate this new life. I still enjoy the smell of freshly shorn fleece, still love to spend time with my dye pots making rainbows of colors to share with the world but cannot commit to shows and schedules. I still do sales when life allows and I can never imagine not working with fibers in any way I can. I keep a drop spindle with some beautiful Rambouillet fleece in my car so any spare moment can still be a spinning moment. Perhaps by the end of the year I'll have mastered the Andean methods of drop spindle spinning and be spinning while I walk.

My best advice to anyone is to not be afraid. Don't be shy or hesitant, you can learn to spin your own yarn, process your own fleece, felt and dye your own product. Resources are available to us like never before with the internet and you can learn all the traditional ways to do things and adapt them to your own life. Dive in there and learn so when the zombie apocalypse comes, you'll be ready to homestead for your family the way our ancestors did.

Email: *bffarts@gmail.com*

Facebook: *www.facebook.com/tamsinjuby/*

YouTube: *http://www.youtube.com/channel/UCtvXgVQrGZpz8S-D8h63yuQ*

### Pauline Campbell - SteampunkSheepYarns

I have always loved knitting and crochet, but after joining Instagram it really took on a different level. I loved knitting socks as it allowed me to try all the lovely indie yarn out there, which led to me dyeing my own. With crochet I wanted to try something different than crocheting my usual blankets, although I do still love making blankets too.

Pauline Campbell from SteampunkSheepYarns.

My Nanny first introduced me to knitting when she was knitting her famous Aran cardigans and Icelandic jumpers for all the family, to keep us warm in the Scottish winters. She bought me my 1st ball of wool, and about 44 years later im still loving it, most of my knitting and crochet is self-taught, and has evolved slowly but gradually to delving deeper into fiber arts, crochet came about 10 years after I learned to knit.

I love anything from the Victorian Era, especially the Industrial age, I also love the sub-culture of Steampunk, which has flavours of an  alternative Victorian style. I also take inspiration from the seasons, especially autumn, and the warm tones, that feature a lot in my yarn dyeing.

I love the process of dyeing as each batch I make is unique, before I dye them I choose the name them after a theme based on Victoriana, once they are dyed, dried and twisted, I then attach a story to them, so that when people are knitting with the yarn, they are taken on a journey through the different tones and shades

For the dyeing, I use citric acid, which helps the fibers to absorb the wool dye, I also use flat aluminium pans to simmer the yarn, another method I use is to steam the yarn, with the crochet I use metal hooks and 100 per cent cotton yarn, as I feel this gives a better structure to my amigurumi. I am most proud of designing some of my crochet dolls, which at the moment I am developing patterns for my Etsy shop.

I have an Etsy shop where I sell my hand-dyed yarn, it is a fairly new project for me so I am still developing it and hope to have a website eventually, I also intend to start selling PDF patterns for my amigurumi.

I work four days a week, but after work I typically come home and aim to be settling down each night crocheting or developing amigurumi patterns. On my days off I batch dye yarn, and create colourways to reflect my themes. I incorporate the traditional craft of needle felting into my amigurumi, using this method to make more realistic eyes, and also hairstyles.

Traditionally crochet thread would be used for doilies/filet work etc, but I use lots of different weights of threads to make outfits and accessories for my amigurumi.

If I were to give advice it would be to try lots of different fiber arts and see what ones suit your time/environment best, I have tried lots of different crafts, and have finally found my niche.

I also love amateur photography, and when taking pics of my yarn for sale, I always try to set the picture up to bring the yarn to life. I also love digital crafting (though basic); I make all my own labels, tags, stitch markers. I have a full leg tattoo that includes balls of wool, and Victorian steampunk images, and my favourite is a steampunk bird pulling a strand of wool from a ball, and it spells out 'nanny'. My beautiful gran who started my love of all things yarn.

### About me:

I'm 52 years old, and married to my biggest supporter, I have two beautiful grandchildren whom I hope to pass on my craft to. I live for my craft and have a craft room in my home, where I will spend hours either taking pics, sorting through my stash to get inspiration or doing papercrafts. No craft is safe and I like to dip in and out of lots of different mediums.

I am an active member on Instagram as (Knitonecrochetone), Etsy as (SteampunkSheepYarns.Etsy.com/) and Facebook which I have just recently started using as SteampunkSheepYarns.

If you have been inspired by the artisans you have read about here – and who could fail to be? – you can 'have a go' at spinning with a drop spindle with a minimum of expenditure. You might even have these items in your crafting kit already!

*You need:*

A wooden car wheel from a craft supplies shop – the type you would use to make a model car. It needs to be around 6–8cm in diameter.

A dowel that fits through the central hole – you need to cut a piece around 25–30cm long.

Hacksaw

Drill

Pencil sharpener

Small jewellery or cup hook

30cm of yarn to use as 'leader' yarn

*What to do:*

1. Drill a hole through the dowel, about 3cm down.
2. Sharpen the undrilled end of the dowel a little with a pencil sharpener. This will help your spindle to spin on a surface when you use it.
3. Screw the hook into the top end of the dowel (the end nearest the drilled hole).
4. Push the bottom (undrilled end) of the dowel piece through the central hole of the wooden wheel. You need to push around 2–3cm through the hole. This will be your whorl.
5. Tie one end of your leader yarn tightly round the dowel just above the whorl (wooden wheel).
6. Take the free end of the yarn over the side of the whorl (wooden wheel) and loop it round the bottom end of the dowel and bring it back up the other side of the whorl.
7. Loop the free end onto the hook, leaving a few centimetres of thread free to start your fibre upon.

*Chapter 12*

# Directory of Suppliers

These suppliers can provide you with everything you need for processing wool, from carders to spinning wheels, spindles and looms, as well as smaller equipment and a wide variety of fibres. A site full of wonderful fibre supplies to make any fibre fan drool – from animal fibre, silk and plant fibres to equipment – everything a spinner could want: *http://www.wildfibres.co.uk*

A large-scale arts and craft supplier with lots available for spinners and weavers including wool carders and spinning wheels: *https://www.georgeweil.com*

Yarn supplier for weavers (and knitters), specialising in ethical silks and recycled sari silks: *https://www.yarnyarn.co.uk*

Buy and sell weaving and spinning equipment and books: *http://www.theloomexchange.co.uk/*

Yarn supplier for weavers, including wholesale quantities: *http://www.fairfieldyarns.co.uk/*

Delicious range of fibres for spinning and felting, including gorgeous gradient sets of shades: *https://www.fellviewfibres.com/*

Supplier of table looms, peg looms, floor looms and weaving accessories: *https://threshingbarn.com/product-category/weaving-supplies/*

Looms, shuttles, spinning wheels, carders and fibres: *https://www.handweavers.co.uk/*

Gorgeous yarns: *http://www.attica-yarns.co.uk/*

US site with suppliers for spinners and weavers as well as lots of useful information: *https://www.yarn.com/pages/weaving*

Wool carder, spinning wheels, looms, fibre and accessories: *https://www.fibrehut.co.uk/*

Fibre, tools and accessories: *http://airedaleyarns.co.uk/*

*Chapter 13*

# Wool and Fibre Festivals

There are a wealth of fibre festivals in the UK, where you can buy wool, yarn and equipment for carding, spinning and weaving. You can watch demonstrations, buy kits and network with knowledgeable fibre artists.

Essex *http://www.walthamabbeywoolshow.co.uk/*

Dornoch, Scottish Highlands *http://www.fibrefest.org.uk/*

Glasgow, Scotland *http://www.stitchandhobby.co.uk/glasgow/spring/*

London *http://www.yarninthecity.com/about-the-yarnporium*

Hertfordshire *http://festiwool.com/*

Nottingham *https://www.nottinghamyarnexpo.com/*

London *https://www.theknittingandstitchingshow.com/london/*

Peak District *https://www.bakewellwool.co.uk/*

Pembrokeshire *https://westwaleswoolshow.weebly.com/*

Cornwall *http://www.3bagsfull.org/*

Loch Ness, Scotland *http://www.lochnessknitfest.com/*

Whitehead, Northern Ireland *https://www.facebook.com/yarnfolkfestivalofwool/*

York *http://britishwool.net/*

Dundee, Scotland *http://ewe.scot/*

Leicester *https://thebigtextileshow.co.uk/*

Kendal *http://www.kendalwoolgathering.co.uk/*

Harrogate *https://www.theknittingandstitchingshow.com/harrogate/*

Berkshire *http://www.southernwoolshow.co.uk/*

Perth *http://perthfestivalofyarn.uk/*

Birmingham *http://www.stitchesandhos.co.uk/yarningham/4591459403*

Bedford *http://www.fibre-east.co.uk/*

Cornwall *http://www.cyfonline.biz/*

Shetland *http://www.shetlandwoolweek.com/*

Skipton *https://yarndale.co.uk/*

Masham, Yorkshire *https://www.mashamsheepfair.com/*

Devon *https://www.facebook.com/southdevonwoolworks/*

Cornwall *http://www.cornwoolly.co.uk/*

Ilkley, West Yorkshire *https://www.wharfewool.co.uk/*

Aberdeen *https://etiom.co.uk/aberdeen-yarnfest*

Staffordshire *http://wool-j13.uk/*

Leeds *www.leeds.gov.uk/museumsandgalleries/armleymills/leeds-wool-festival*

Norfolk *https://worsteadweavers.org.uk/woolly-worstead-2018/*

Cockermouth, Cumbria *https://www.woolfest.co.uk/*

*Chapter 14*

# Training Courses and Spinning Guilds

There are a huge – and growing – number of day courses and residential courses available, should you wish to learn to spin or weave. Here is a selection:

Learn to hand spin on a traditional hill farm in the Brecon Beacons National Park. Courses in animal husbandry, spinning, weaving and acid dyeing in Powys. Also courses in spinning exotic yarns such as yak, cashmere, Kevlar, rose and bamboo. *https://www.allinaspin.co.uk/workshops-courses/*

Learn to spin and weave in Bolton, in the North West.
*https://janeflanagantextiles.co.uk/*

Learn to weave in Somerset.
*http://www.janetphillips-weaving.co.uk/*

Create with Fibre – learn to spin, weave and dye fibre in East Ayrshire and beyond. *http://createwithfibre.co.uk/*

Learn to weave with instructor Lindsey Campbell. Beginner and intermediate online video weaving classes. Online courses.
*https://www.hellohydrangea.com/weaving-classes*
*https://www.craftsy.com/*

**Spinning Guilds**
Walsall Handspinners and Weavers
*http://myweb.tiscali.co.uk/walsallhandspinners/*

Swansea and Neath Port Talbot, Wales, UK
Tawe Guild of Weavers, Spinners and Dyers
*http://taweguildofweaversspinnersdyers.blogspot.co.uk/*

Alsager, Cheshire, UK
Alsager Guild of Weavers, Spinners and Dyers
*http://www.alsagerwsd.co.uk/*

North Wales, UK
Abergele Guild of Weavers, spinners and dyers
*http://abergelewsd.blogspot.co.uk/*

West Sussex, UK
West Sussex Guild of Weavers, Spinners and Dyers
*https://wsgwsd.wordpress.com/*

Nottingham, UK
Ashfield Guild of Spinners, Weavers and Dyers.
*http://ashfieldguild.btck.co.uk/*

Norwich, North Norfolk, UK
Worstead Guild of Weavers, Spinners & Dyers
*https://worsteadweavers.org.uk/*

Cumbria, UK
Eden Valley Guild of Spinners, Weavers and Dyers
*https://edenvalleyguild.co.uk/*

Cornwall, UK
Cornwall Guild of Weavers Spinners & Dyers
http://cgwsd.weebly.com/

# Chapter 15

# Useful Books and Websites

Here is a list of interesting and informative books to help you explore the world of spinning and weaving further.

**Baines, Patricia.** *Flax and Linen.* Shire, 1985

**Baines, Patricia.** *Linen: Hand Spinning and Weaving.* Batsford, 1989

**Walsh, Penny.** *Spinning, Dyeing and Weaving* Self Sufficiency, 2009

**Kroll, Carol.** *The Whole Craft of Spinning: From the Raw Material to the Finished Yarn.* Dover, 2003

**Franquemont, Abby.** *Respect the Spindle.* Interweave, 2009

**Amos, Alden.** *Big Book of Handspinning.* Interweave, 2001

**Martineau, Ashley.** *Spinning and Dyeing Yarn: The Home Spinner's Guide to Creating Traditional and Yarn Art.* Jacqui Small LLP 2014

**Moreno, Jillian.** *Yarnitecture.* Storey Publishing, 2016

**Anderson, Sarah.** *Spinner's Book of Yarn Designs.* Storey Publishing, 2013

**Robson, Deborah and Ekarius, Carol.** *Fleece and Fiber Sourcebook.* Storey, 2011

**Robson, Deborah.** *The Field Guide to Fleece.* Storey Books, 2013

**Field, Anne.** *Learn to Spin: With Anne Field.* Search Press Ltd, 2011

**Field, Anne.** *Spinning Wool.* A&C Black Publishers Ltd, 2011

**Smith, Beth.** *The Spinner's Book of Fleece.* Storey Publishing, 2014

**Casey, Maggie.** *Start Spinning: Everything You Need to Know to Make Great Yarn.* Interweave, 2008

**Patrick, Jane.** *Weaver's Idea Book: Creative Cloth on a Rigid-Heddle Loom* Interweave, 2010

**Patrick, Jane.** *Woven Scarves: 26 Inspired Designs for the Rigid Heddle Loom.* Interweave, 2014

**Strutt, Laura.** *Modern Weaving: Learn to weave with 25 bright and brilliant loom weaving projects.* CICO Books, 2016

**Moodie, Maryanne.** *On the Loom: A Modern Weaver's Guide.* Abrams Books, 2016

**Davenport, Betty Linn.** *Hands on Rigid Heddle Weaving.* Interweave, 1987

**Ross, Lynn Gray.** *Hand Weaving: The Basics.* Bloomsbury Visual Arts, 2014

**Glasbrook, Kirsten.** *Tapestry Weaving.* Search Press Classics, 2015

**Mitchell, Syne.** *Inventive Weaving on a Little Loom.* Storey Publishing, 2015

**Dixon, Anne.** *Handweaver's Pattern Book: An Illustrated Reference to Over 600 Fabric Weaves.* A&C Black Publishers Ltd, 2007

**Chandler, Deborah.** *Learning to Weave.* Interweave, 2009

**Richards, Anne.** *Weaving Textiles That Shape Themselves.* The Crowood Press Ltd, 2012

**Kearley, Sharon.** *Woven Textiles: A Designer's Guide.* The Crowood Press Ltd, 2014

**Shenton, Jan.** *Woven Textile Design.* Laurence King, 2014

**Graver, Pattie.** *Next Steps in Weaving: What You Never Knew You Needed to Know.* Interweave, 2015

## Useful Websites

These websites are links to a variety of helpful and informative information about spinning, weaving and the textile industry in general.

Website of the Association of Guilds of Weavers, Spinners and Dyers – dedicated to the 'preservation and improvement of the craftsmanship in hand weaving, spinning and dyeing.' The perfect place to find out about guild membership, courses and more. *http://www.wsd.org.uk/*

Affiliated to the Association of Guilds of Weavers, Spinners and Dyers, the online guild was established in 2002 for those fibre and textile artists who could not attend guild meetings in person. *http://www. onlineguildwsd.org.uk/*

Excellent website about cotton and cotton weaving *https://www. englishfinecottons.co.uk/*

A brilliant historic and archaeological resource about textiles *https:// pallia.net/en/*

Website of the sumptuous and fascinating magazine, *Selvedge* with lots of information about spinning and weaving among other fabric-related topics. A cornucopia of textile-based loveliness. *https://www.selvedge. org/blogs/selvedge/spinning-and-weaving*

Fantastic history blog. *https://comestepbackintime.wordpress.com/tag/ tudor-weaving-in-southampton/*

Massive amount of information and books/products to purchase. *http:// www.e-weaving.com/*

National Trust owned textiles mill near Manchester. You can explore the mill itself (and buy fabric woven there); find out about the conditions that mill workers lived in, in their purpose-built tied cottages and contract this with Quarry Bank House, lived in by the rich mill owner, Samuel Greg and his family. *https://www.nationaltrust. org.uk/quarry-bank*

A magazine for hand spinning that has ceased production, yet many great resources and information on the site. *http://www.yarnmaker.co.uk/*

A supplier with a great set of learning resources for spinning and weaving. *https://www.weaversbazaar.com*

An interesting film about The London Cloth Company, established in 2011. They use traditional weaving techniques and refurbished equipment dating back to the 1870s. Some very interesting ideas about using traditional methods in the modern day. *http://www.bbc.co.uk/news/av/magazine-26179200/weaving-modern-cloth-with-victorian-looms*

Raising silk worms for an arts project. *https://thesilkwormstakehalifax.wordpress.com/*

Interesting website with information about different types of spinning wheel. *http://www.ukspinningwheels.info/*

British Pathé News film on 'How Fibres are Spun'. *https://www.youtube.com/watch?v=pLtdyFIe_VA*

British Pathé News film on loom weaving. *http://www.britishpathe.com/video/weaving-1/*

BFI film from 1957 about linen weaving. *https://player.bfi.org.uk/free/film/watch-linen-weaving-1957-online*

Watch Axminster wool carpets being woven. *https://www.youtube.com/watch?v=QmHPTd4qXUM*

Textile Museum. *https://www.textielmuseum.nl*

History of linen production in Ireland. *https://www.fergusonsirishlinen.com/pages/index.asp?title2=history-of-irish-linen&title1=about-linen*

Fascinating resource about ethically run and fairtrade spinning and weaving projects around the world. *http://weavearealpeace.org/artisan-resource-guide/*

Senegalese artisanal weaving. *http://www.lionessesofafrica.com/blog/2014/10/27/video-artisan-weaving-craft-of-senegal*

# Index